RESEARCH

ACTION RESEARCH

A Practical Guide for Transforming Your School Library

Judith A. Sykes

2002
LIBRARIES UNLIMITED
A Division of Greenwood Publishing Group, Inc.
Greenwood Village, Colorado

This book is dedicated to Dr. Joseph T. Pascarelli,
a professor at the School of Education at
the University of Portland in Oregon, who taught, guided,
and inspired me to understand
research in a transformational context.

■■■■■■■■■■■■■■■■■■■■■■■■■■■■■■■■■

Libraries Unlimited
A Division of Greenwood Publishing Group, Inc.
7730 East Belleview Ave., Suite A200
Greenwood Village, CO 80111
1-800-237-6124
www.lu.com

Library of Congress Cataloging-in-Publication Data

Sykes, Judith A., 1957-
    Action research : a practical guide for transforming your school library / Judith A. Sykes.
        p. cm.
    Includes bibliographical references and index.
    ISBN 1-56308-875-4
    1. School libraries--Research--Methodology. 2. Action research in education. I. Title.

Z675.S3 S955 2002
027.8'07--dc21

                                                                    2001050537

Contents

PART I: An Action Research Journey

PART II: Presentation (also on CD-ROM)

Foreword

The springboard for Ms. Sykes's reflection and action research was a hunch that libraries, one of the last democratic institutions to foster quality learning, were somewhat out of step with the present and less ready for the future than they should be. This led her on a journey of action research—a process by which she gave careful consideration to her beliefs and assumptions about the power of libraries in our culture. Through reflection and sustained inquiry, she presents readers with both a model and a challenge to transform libraries so they become more central in the lives of children, youth, and communities.

She is successful in making new meaning for us in terms of the potential of libraries in our culture. Using her own firsthand experiences as a professional librarian-educator; her sense of professional inquiry, which is the hallmark of every growing professional; a group of colleagues and experts in the field; and her willingness to engage in intentional reflection, she presents to us a pathway to transform libraries as they reshape to meet the future.

The intent of action research is to enable the professional to "live in a question" for a period of time and ultimately define ways to improve practice. Ms. Sykes has transcended this and gone beyond her own practice in her school district. She offers keen insight into the challenge of reshaping the institution of the library so that it becomes aligned with our present needs and is able to anticipate and respond to the future. It is clear that throughout her work, like all action researchers, she has strengthened her own sense of advocacy and allows learners of all ages to recognize that libraries are at the core of a learning society.

Joseph T. Pascarelli, Ed.D.
Associate Professor
University of Portland

Preface

Many teacher-librarians or school library media specialists constantly advocate, strive, or, indeed, struggle, to keep their school libraries open and alive. As success stories surface and begin to inspire, we hear other stories about school libraries locking their doors. In speaking with individual teacher-librarians, teacher-librarian groups or associations, and school library and other educational personnel at district levels, I discovered a need—now more than ever—for teacher-librarians (school library media specialists) to reach out to their constituents to build shared understanding of the impact of school libraries on student learning.

Many of these busy professionals, tired of years of traditional advocating and fighting for their programs, can find the model of the action research process in this book beneficial by replicating the process. Or, after reading about my journey, individuals can adapt the process or presentation to their current needs. This qualitative research process, familiar to academia, can lend itself to practical approaches by enabling teacher-librarians to transform their school libraries and research programs. Many educators are keen on this "new" research process but are unsure of how to approach or engage in it at the school level. This book's purpose is to present, through my journey and findings, a model for using this process.

In a recent newsletter from the International Association of School Librarianship (IASL), President Blanche Woolls wrote about the miracles needed to help increase worldwide literacy involving school libraries: "It may be that a presentation at a meeting that has been planned will be more successful than trying to plan such a meeting." This book also provides a presentation model that teacher-librarians could use or adapt in building understanding about individual or district school libraries.

I developed this book as the exit project for my University of Portland master's degree in educational leadership. I am grateful to the university for the efforts and excellence in teaching and learning inspired by each professor in a program where each course built upon the foundations from the previous one. Woven throughout the program was the eventual outcome of an exit project involving action research.

The professor who taught the "Teacher As Researcher" course, Dr. Joseph Pascarelli, guided and facilitated my growth as a professional to realms which seem to know no boundaries. This exuberant, enthusiastic professor challenged our preconceived notions of research and leadership with the action research process. Prior to this course, "action research" seemed like another educational buzzword. For me, it has now become a way to approach life! Learning is never finished; it is enriched and inspired, and it travels in new directions. During the learning process, I never hesitated to contact Dr. Pascarelli by phone, fax, or e-mail for additional insight and tutelage. Sometimes, the responses were lengthy. Other times, Dr. Pascarelli would give a sentence or a nudge in the right direction, and I was off again. Through this modeling, I have changed my approach to classroom teaching as well as the work I do with adults and staff in conducting presentations and in-services.

As the former school library evaluation specialist for the Calgary Board of Education—Canada's second largest board, with 225 schools—I remember telling Dr. Pascarelli that there were very few "experts" in my area to contact for my research. School libraries were in crisis. His response: Call the Canadian Library Association, the American Library Association, deans of school libraries all over the world, authors in the field, and so on. Dr. Pascarelli encouraged me to apply for a grant, which I received, from my board's staff development department. New worlds and connections suddenly opened up to me, and I now hold executive positions in associations and am in my third term as president of the Association of Teacher-Librarianship of Canada.

Dr. Pascarelli continued to support my work and growth throughout my research. Although I felt I had never worked harder, I enjoyed it a lot and learned much. A "snowball" effect ensued as my research led to an appointment in my school board as co-chair of the Future of School Libraries Task Force. Finally, Dr. Pascarelli encouraged me to publish this project.

I recall feeling despondent one evening in class. There were so many cut-backs in school libraries. Dr. Pascarelli then reminded us about something very important: "Remember who you are, what you believe in, what you have accomplished. Share your voice and self-confidence." Reflected in the words of Walt Crawford and Michael Gorman, we should "take pride in the way librarians have honored this mission for centuries and accept the weight of that mission" (1994).

In my own experience, the action research process strengthened my participation and voice as a member of my school board's Future of School Libraries Task Force. This task force eventually developed a document called *School Libraries Supporting Quality Learning* (Calgary, Alberta: Calgary Board of Education, 1999). This document has gone to operational policy committees and trustees for approval and guidelines for implementation. Learning how to see the world through a researcher's eyes and articulate my own findings and conclusions through presentations enabled me to lead this task force.

During the process of my research, I gained support from the Professional Learning Support Department and the then staff development department of the Calgary Board of Education. Directors Jim Latimer and Dariel Bateman were also there for me in person, or by phone, fax, or e-mail, for discussion, questions, insight, and tutelage. At that time, the staff development department had also begun an initiative for educators in various fields who were experimenting with action research with start-up grants, focus groups, book studies, and forums for sharing what one experienced during the stages of action research. Some of us formally used action research through university programs, while others explored action research directly from the classroom. Together, we learned about the transformational aspects of action research and their enabling impact on education.

The first part of this book presents an outline of the key elements of the action research process. It is told through the story of my journey into examining the future of school libraries. Tips are given throughout for adapting the process to schools, and additional chapters suggest strategies for developing a school library vision and a third-grade project.

The second part of the book includes a ready-made presentation that readers can either deliver by making overhead transparencies or by using the CD-ROM. Teacher-librarians could use this presentation right away with their staff, administrators, parent councils, or school boards to build shared understanding about school libraries and the potential for their future. Other readers might wish to adapt the model to their own research themes, such as exploring virtual libraries or diversity and the school library.

Acknowledgments

I would like to thank the University of Portland (Oregon) for the opportunity to conduct my graduate work in the realms of action research and the future of school libraries.

I would also like to thank the Calgary Board of Education, specifically the original Future of School Libraries Task Force, initiated and supported by Chief Superintendent Dr. Donna Michaels. Likewise, the leadership, support, and encouragement I received from Jim Latimer, director of Program/Professional Learning Support, and Dariel Bateman, director of Staff Development, was invaluable. I thank them and all the task force members and stakeholder group members for believing in my research, working with me, and guiding me; for supporting me with not only a financial grant that enabled me to engage a student task force but also for presenting me with a myriad of opportunities to grow as a reflective practitioner in this look at the future.

Introduction

Through this book, the reader will experience my journey into and findings about action research exploring the future of school libraries. Prior to that unfolding journey, a brief introduction to the process of action research is in order.

What is action research? Teacher-librarians/school library media specialists will find that many parts in the action research process are familiar to them as components of traditional research processes used daily with students. What is unique about action research is that it gives researchers—teachers or students—the dimensions of actively doing and applying research to their own worlds in a personal, reflective growth pattern. Researchers are in the driver's seat, studying their own school and community. Researchers parallel the working modalities of the scientist or investigator, interacting with others and constructing deep meaning about the topic, making new discoveries, and challenging their own ideas and opinions. This is not a neatly packaged process. Many twists and turns can occur and take the researcher from one idea to another, changing his or her thinking on the topic. Action research is grounded in the principles of the American Educational Research Association [AERA] and the American Psychology Association [APA].

What can this process look like? Once they consider a topic for research, researchers record all previous knowledge they might have on the topic and write about what they know or assume to know about the topic using a graphic organizer, such as a web, chart, or list. Like scientists, researchers will test and focus in on their preconceptions as they research. From these notations, researchers carefully develop a series of questions, followed by a list of all possible resources, including people, that will inform the research.

Researchers must now establish **context** to create a focus for the size and scope of the research. Like the setting for a play or story: How broad will the study sweep? What are the demographics? Will it focus on a single event or project? A classroom? The school library? Several classrooms? An entire school? Other school libraries? A school district? What aspect(s) of the researcher's own work will it encompass?

Once researchers have framed the research demographically and topically, they study the questions they put forth on the topic. One question or part of the topic might clearly stand out; this most important question can be known as the researcher's **issue**. Unlike a traditional hypothesis, an issue can become the underpinning of vision. It can be based on a hunch or a thought that researchers have concerning the topic, thus the research evolves. It is a question that they will come back to and search for in the research that might lead them to other information they had not thought about. It is a question that keeps researchers interested in knowing more. Researchers keep the issue in mind at all times as they continue with the research.

Researchers of an issue must be well-versed in its current literature and in the literature of the field. A literature review relevant to the researcher's key issue will build upon the researcher's background and develop insight into the topic. Researchers can conduct this review through various means: professional or university libraries, public libraries, or virtual libraries. Internet sites, such as AskERIC, host a team of voluntary graduate students who will assist with a literature review free of charge and e-mail a resulting bibliography that can help researchers to identify key literature in their field. Current literature in the field can update researchers on developments or knowledge about the topic. Researchers should consider all sources: books, professional journals, the Internet, professional videos, brochures, and pamphlets. The literature review will also help researchers identify experts in the field.

Researchers use the literature review to decide if what they read or learned from it informed their own quests. Did they come up with new directions? They can now make some informed decisions about where they are going to focus their writing and research and can compose these decisions as **goals**. Most researchers will focus on one or two key goals and, from these goals, decide exactly what they will try to achieve—what the research **outcomes** could be—in the realms of the topic by studying their own situations. Looking back at their initial preconceptions and newly written goals/outcomes, researchers create a **plan** for what the components of the study's next stages will be and who needs to be involved, developing their own planning model for an approach to gathering data. Who needs to be involved? Students? Parents? Colleagues? Will the researchers contact experts in the field? In what key questions or activities will they involve others? What tools or events will be used to involve them? Such tools or techniques of gathering data include interviews (telephone, e-mail, in person, focus groups, surveys, audiotape, or videotape) or events where researchers are participant-observers who keep a reflective journal to document the events in which they participate. Most researchers will use a variety of at least three techniques or tools such as what follows in this book. For further details, researchers are referred to sources such as *Studying Your Own School: An Educator's Guide to Qualitative Practitioner Research* by Gary L. Anderson, Kathryn Herr, and Ann Sigrid Nihlen.

As researchers move into their own research events, descriptive recordings about each event take form as field notes. These notes contain the dates, times, locations, people involved, and other details about the event. They are an account of the events where researchers attempt some reconstruction of dialogue and records of their own reflections. Researchers then analyze these field notes.

This analysis involves coding the data and circling or highlighting key words and phrases occurring in all of the events that will lead researchers to **patterns** or **themes** to construct meaning around their questions. The researchers look for what seems to be common about the topic, no matter where or whom they read, saw, or heard about it from. When they find at least one or two of these key patterns or themes, they develop **conclusions** to frame the research. The action research results are discussed, and the research reflects on changes or findings based on the data.

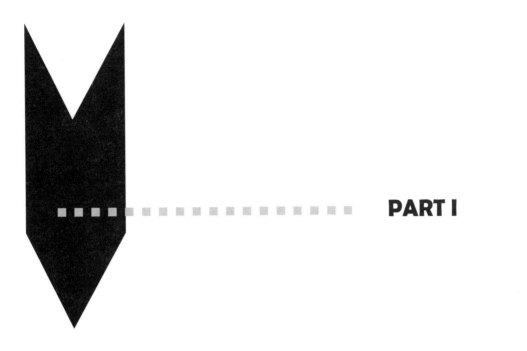

PART I

An Action Research Journey

CHAPTER 1

Establishing Context

The process of putting my research into motion—beginning an action research journey—necessitated making a decision regarding the scope and focus of the work into which I would immerse myself. The school library field is immense. Where would I best begin this journey—the point of departure to reflection and study in work I had done for more than a decade? It was like creating the setting for a play or story: How broad could the study sweep? Would it focus on a single event or project? A classroom? Several classrooms? A school? A school district? What would the demographics encompass? What aspect(s) of my own work would I explore?

Initially, I thought about furthering studies in that critical domain of my work in school libraries: information literacy. I also thought about looking at learning resources and how they continue to evolve through new and advancing technologies. As I reflected extensively on so many recent conversations I had had with colleagues in school libraries, the issue that kept arising was not the excitement of working with students, information literacy, resources, or teachers but the realities of the decimation of school libraries in this era of information and communication technologies!

What was going on? Would we need books, or would computers and the Internet replace them and us? School library personnel were having their hours reduced or were being laid off or assigned to other classroom duties in an increasing manner. Would there be a future for school libraries? I thus decided to focus on the very heart of the matter: the future for school libraries. Were we ahead of our time in educational design and practices, or did we need to change? If so, how? What was happening to school libraries and why?

Thus, transforming school libraries presented a broad and global theme in which to set a context. I discovered that many associations and agencies around the world work diligently at supporting school libraries. The International Association of School Librarianship (IASL) actively addresses issues related to school libraries globally. In the United States, a national symposium produced "Information Power" (ALA, 1988) for school libraries which resulted in a collaboration between the American Association of School Libraries and the Association of Educational Communications and Technologies to produce national standards for information literacy. In Canada, a national symposium on information, literacy, and the school library involving stakeholders from education, parents, and business communities took place in Ottawa in November 1997.[1]

I proceeded to look closer to home. In Canada, curriculum development is not centralized but localized through each provincial government. Therefore, I contacted Alberta Education about future directions for school libraries in that province. The response I received was that individual school boards in Alberta would be responsible for funding and staffing school libraries. I was encouraged to work with my local school board and other groups involved in school libraries to discover what lay in the future for school libraries. Therefore, the context of my journey became anchored within a large metropolitan public school system.

→ TIP: You might wish to consider the policies on school libraries in your jurisdiction, or set the context for transformation within your school library in your own school.

My school system is divided into five superintendencies and eight smaller "collaborative learning communities"—areas encompassing 25 to 30 schools that range from kindergarten through senior high. These "families" of schools focus on common issues. One of the five superintendencies supports curriculum so at the time of this journey my role in the unit of curriculum involved resource evaluation and selection as a specialist providing support to schools and school libraries.

→ TIP: Consider the role you have in your school or school community. What services do you provide? What beliefs drive those services in your day-to-day work?

My day-to-day work in this journey involved providing lists of recommended resources in all formats for school library collection development. This included resources for respecting the diversity of all learners in every curriculum, grade, learning style, and in second languages, primarily French. As my journey began, the Alberta government mandated that all school boards in the province submit a technology plan. Virtual schools or libraries were not yet on the forefront—they were in the very developmental stages of talk. I joined with my school library colleagues in feeling pressured about this technology plan. I wondered if school libraries would be a part of it all or if they would continue to erode, disappear, or become computer labs. I knew that as a teacher-librarian, other teacher-librarians and I had often led the way in learning and teaching with technology. Many of us banded together to voice these concerns, and an outcome was the creation of a Future of School Libraries Task Force, formed by my chief superintendent at the time. I was selected as a member of the task force and have co-chaired it ever since. The task force provided me with another contextual experience for my journey, which would involve researching, observing, and reflecting upon the issue of the future of school libraries.

➡️ TIP: You can replicate the following macro-study on a smaller scale within your school library with staff and students or within your larger school community involving parents and other key stakeholders.

How does one study the future? As I began to prepare to study the future of school libraries, I became a participant-observer in the journey of action research. Many opportunities arose to participate in events and dialogue relating to the future of school libraries. I could then step back and reflect—both in preparing background and looking ahead. Wherever I went or whatever I did—school library meetings, a library assistant network group, task force meetings, department meetings, school library visits, association meetings, professional reading—I began a notebook detailing comments, concerns, and frustrations relating to the future of school libraries. This very messy notebook would become an integral part of the journey from which I would develop structures and design my own tools for research as well as my own model of understanding.

➡ TIP: It is critical to keep a notebook or journal as you engage in the process of action research. This does not have to be formal; you can jot down a few key statements, recommendations, and leads for further reflection or use. Remember to date all entries, and record names and contact information. These will prove very useful as you move into the next stages of action research. These are also known as field notes. An example of notes follows with a chart that you can copy.

FIELD NOTES—SAMPLE CHART

Date: *September 7*

Event: *Teleconference*

DESCRIPTION	METHOD	ANALYSIS
An account of an event. • Who was there? (portraits) Can you reconstruct any of the dialogue? The physical setting? Your behavior? *Perceptions?* • My first conference call as a member of the board of directors of the Association for Teacher-Librarianship in Canada (ATLC) • Physical setting involved strictly listening; I was able to comment on a few of the items of business; others held the conversation much longer. • Members were from all over the country and with vast experiences in school libraries. • Much discussion about advocacy.	*How did you go about the event?* • I had volunteered to edit the association's journal and take part in association events.	*Construct your meaning of the event.* • I will learn a lot from members who have been involved in national activities for a long time. • I can compare my local musings with other parts of the country. • I can try a variety of advocacy methods that I have not tried before, such as a focus group where participants can write a definition of future libraries together. **Contacts:** • Must e-mail ATLC president to request an interview.

FIELD NOTES CHART

Date:

Event:

DESCRIPTION	METHOD	ANALYSIS
An account of an event.	*How did you go about the event?*	*Construct your meaning of the event.*
Perceptions?		**Contacts:**

Note

1.   The symposium continued in Toronto in June 1999, where attendees outlined goals for national work and formed a "Vision 2020" national committee composed of representatives from Canada's two national library associations: The Association for Teacher-Librarianship of Canada (ATLC) and the Canadian School Library Association (CSLA). It will attempt to unite provincial, territorial, and other educational organizations in establishing national school library standards.

CHAPTER 2

The Issue

Now that I had a context for my journey into the future of school libraries, I needed to decide on a focus—a key issue or problem to investigate in action research. Instead of a traditional hypothesis, I was encouraged to think about this issue as the underpinning of a vision I might develop regarding the transformation of future school libraries—a "hunch" I might have as to the direction of future school libraries.

I had a hunch that future school libraries would be vital centers of constructivist learning in both real and virtual time. For a long time, I thought that school libraries needed to move from current practices and models to facilitate constructivist models. I read about what we know and continue to learn about the brain, then reflected upon this new learning with past use and understanding of resource-based learning, information literacy, and cooperative learning techniques from my school library programs. School libraries, I envisioned, would be places— both real and virtual—for human connection, inquiry, and literacy development.

I had a hunch that school libraries would be central to schools as learning laboratories, having an impact on and enhancing teacher and student growth and knowledge. Projects would intertwine with curriculum as students became immersed in the inquiry process and teachers guided them as coaches, facilitators, and critical friends. School libraries would serve to create independent, lifelong learners who could reflect upon knowledge from print, media, and human sources to make new meanings for themselves and enhance the application and communication of their learning. These students would seek to understand and be understood in an environment where "viewpoints are presented objectively and materials are available without cost of purchase" (Crawford and Gorman, 1994).

My hunch continued. I pictured school libraries as places of active learning that exemplify the definition of collaboration among all stakeholders—foundational aspects of school improvement plans and whole-school culture. Equity of access to quality resources and programs must occur within this culture and across it to other schools and the global community. Educators need to facilitate this process in a spirit of inclusion where diversity in culture, learning styles, personality styles, intelligence, and energy levels is honored in the learning process.

Information abounds in all formats; known ones, such as print, audio, and video, evolve and even merge with new formats, such as CD-ROM and the Internet. Formats that are not yet invented or are in their early stages, such as virtual reality, will be part of our children's future learning resources. As my hunch unfolded, I knew that qualified teacher-librarians would be vital to the transformation of future school libraries providing expertise and a link between students, teachers, and learning with information of all types.

I could not look any further into the excitement of the unfolding vision until I discovered, if possible, why the understanding of such a vision was not shared by stakeholders or decision-makers in the field. Everyone seemed to state that he or she "loved libraries," so why were school libraries understaffed, under-funded, or closed? And, moreover, what could be done about it?

➤ TIP: What is the "burning issue" in your school or school board? Is it similar? Or is there something else that drives your inquiry state—something that you need deeper learning about?

CHAPTER 3

Current Literature

My journey's next stage involved exploring current literature in the field. To study the future of school libraries, I needed to read futurists on the burgeoning global information and communication era. My literature review needed to highlight those works that were most influential to my journey.

In a profession feeling the effects of change and cutbacks now more than ever, authors Walt Crawford and Michael Gorman (1994) state that librarians wishing to embrace the future must "remember that human service to human beings is their prime reason for existing" (p. 182). Knowledge and understanding, not data and information, are central to the mission of equality of access to materials and resources for all. We should "take pride in the way librarians have honored this mission for centuries, and accept the weight of that mission" (p. 182). Crawford and Gorman point out that Mortimer Adler referred to four "goods of the mind" on a scale from least value to greatest value. Information for information's sake is of least value to a society, whereas, with knowledge, data is transformed into meaning. Meaning transforms into understanding of the worldview and personal perspectives. This, in turn, leads to wisdom, where understanding is whole and generative.

Librarians need to take pride in their name; those seeking to change to something like "information specialist" oversimplify the role. Let's hope our doctor or mechanic is an "information specialist" in their field. Librarians have their own mission: the preservation and availability of all forms of human communication organized with some clarity and thought. Crawford and Gorman (1994) argue that no matter what format knowledge is in, libraries retain the best of the past so that we are not condemned to repeat catastrophes. Furthermore, they point out a balance between the worlds of print and electronic resources—formats come and go, so many libraries can become museums of dead technologies: the filmstrip, 16mm film, etc.—and warn us about the effects of "technolust" (p. 36–52). Crawford and Gorman state that "libraries are about empowering the unempowered through knowledge and information, not about participating in the distribution of an electronic opiate of the people" (p. 128). Humans need time to organize, analyze, synthesize, and create. Libraries work toward an equitable society through universal literacy. As the Canadian Library Association states in the 1998 draft for its strategic plan, "libraries and the principals of intellectual freedom and free universal access to information are key components of an open and democratic society" (p. 5).

Futurists write that citizens of tomorrow must become adept questioners and critical users of information. Nicholas Negroponte (1995) discusses the digital world as requiring new thinking processes needing to be developed as new technologies emerge. Even the book, revered for its ability to be read in bed, on the bus, and so forth, might have a digital counterpart of similar size, cost, portability, and interactivity in the not-too-distant future. Derrick de Kerckhove (1995) tells us that we will need to move from hierarchical, competitive societies to supportive, collaborative, interactive cultures. He further elaborates that in the future touch might become our most important cognitive tool. Simulated tactility, or "virtual reality," might be powerful enough to take us out of the literal, frontal mindset based on the alphabet and allow us to store information the way the mind stores it. This will take us from being "Homo theoreticus" to "Homo participans" as the gap between technology and psychology narrows. These technologies will empower individuals as the economy moves from producer-driven to consumer-driven. We need enlightened access to all formats of resources for resource-based learning—formats that speak to different learning styles. Viewing television is often one-dimensional, while computers are interactive; print is linear, allowing for reflection.

David Shenk (1996) suggests a definition of education for the information age: "Would that learning were as easy as diving into a swimming pool of information or sitting down to a banquet table for an info-feast. Rather, education, which comes from the Latin *educare*, meaning to raise and nurture, is more a matter of imparting values and critical faculties than inputting raw data. Education is about enlightenment, not just access" (p. 202–3). Shenk maps out the effects on society and the individual of today's overabundance of information. The more we know, the less we know, or as Shenk puts it: "We face a paradox of abundance-induced amnesia" (p. 124). Shenk describes information as a "natural resource" needing to be managed more than acquired; what we need is not so much news but shared understandings. He urges educators to embrace the teaching of information literacy so that the quality of our thinking is as great as the quantity of our information.

According to Donald Hamilton (1994), the school library's collection is the "stuff of the mission, the catalyst for the instruction . . . the raw material for the education laboratory that is the school" (p. 24). It is crucial to have personnel who have insight into the complexity of collection development. Without educators in place in the school library, who will search for the best? The daily papers, the Sunday review sections, and the weekly or monthly magazines pay children's resources halfhearted, impossibly delayed, or "months after they were published" reviews— few outside the insular children's book world have heard about the evolution of some of the most interesting art forms of our time: the 32-page picture book, the heavily illustrated nonfiction text, the young adult novel (Aronson 1997, p. 428). Gail Edwards (1996) spoke about the need for schools to look for resources that promote "ideals" such as anti-racism or literature that will extend student experiences to teach critical thinking and tolerance rather than censor. It's how we use the material that is key; how we challenge attitudes in them.

As touch becomes the cognitive tool for the future, Jamie McKenzie (1997b) tells us "the question may be the most powerful technological tool we have ever created." The kinds of questions we ask and guide our students in asking should reach for essential truths. McKenzie recommends a "questioning toolbox" be placed next to every computer station in K–12. We must encourage students to develop "telling questions"; to explore raw data, then compare it to a topic; and to build meaning from telling questions. After all, authentic research explores the unknown. McKenzie (1997b) proposed a cyclic research model: question-plan-gather-sort and sift-synthesize-evaluate-report. After several repetitions of the cycle, the researcher can develop insight. McKenzie (1996b) also urges planning for future school libraries that are flexible and open, preparing lifelong learners for their future and not this generation's past.

This shift in the educational paradigm requires resources needed to engage and promote growth, develop critical literacies in learners, and organize the information glut or push. As McKenzie (1997a) points out, reading will change in two ways: breadth and depth. Students need to make answers, not find them, to change the traditional research paradigm. We are challenged to take our students beyond the "info-glut, info-tactics Toffler identified, the 'eye/mind candy' tainted with entertainment and advertising," into deeper thinking and deeper reading. "Mind bytes" on the Internet might give a student a two-minute look at a topic such as euthanasia. Many of the better web sites, such as Electric Library, are not free. McKenzie, the recent director of Libraries, Media, and Technology at Bellingham, Washington Public Schools, increased school library budgets by 50 percent to update badly dated print collections and purchase new books or the better web sites that are not free. Students need to be prepared to use good judgment using resources, developing "information power over the information merchants" with a balance of information delivery systems, such as the Internet, books, lectures, and texts.

There is a vast realm of research with which those working in school libraries and beyond the field need to develop familiarity. Ken Haycock (1998) and Dianne Oberg (1997) both state that the "Colorado Study" (Lance, et al., 1993), which demonstrated that schools with excellent libraries scored the highest on statewide achievement tests, is the research study most often quoted and known. But Haycock (1997) tells us that there are more than 30 years of research and more than 600 dissertations on the impact of effective school library programs on achievement scores when teachers and teacher-librarians collaborate. The evidence is there, but as Haycock points out, school library experiences are best remembered by personal experience. Most educators and decision-makers most recently remember their secondary library from their past rather than the constructivist environment needed for the digital generation. The role of school libraries must be noted as quite different than other libraries that could be mostly providing physical access to information rather than intellectual access to information or the student's ability to process and use information effectively (p. 49).

Haycock relates that industry, in reports such as the U.S. SCANS report, refer to future employees having the ability to use resources, manage information, work in groups, use systems, and understand technologies. He also reports that there are key initiatives supporting the school library of the future in the United States.

In Chicago, schools had openings in 1997 for more than 100 full-time teacher-librarians but could not locate sufficiently qualified personnel. That same year in Los Angeles, state departments of education redirected $5.3 million to elementary schools to revitalize their school libraries due to declining reading scores. The state of Arkansas requires a full-time teacher-librarian to improve student achievement. The Dewitt Wallace Foundation provided $43 million for school library partnerships, which Haycock states is the largest nongovernmental school reform effort in American history. Haycock recommends essential discussions in educational and library communities to resolve conflicting perceptions and frameworks around school libraries.

David Loertscher (1996) views the school library program of the future as needing to be more student-centered in developing information literacy so that students become "avid readers, critical and creative thinkers, interested learners, organized investigators, effective communicators, responsible information users, and skilled users of technology" (p. 192–93). We need to present many different information literacy models so that learners can internalize them and create their own inquiry models. By sixth grade, students should thus be able to discuss which model or process they used, if presented with a number over the years. Teacher-librarians need to lead the process as professional development experts connecting to learning. School libraries of the future will need to change to meet specialty schools, charter schools, home-schools, and other scenarios (Loertscher, 1995). The "tools of learning" in their various formats do not "jump out at students and automatically make a difference without an intermediary—the library media specialist" (p. 90).

Doug Johnson (1997) emphasizes that "classrooms and media centers need to work together to make our children better citizens, better consumers, better communicators, better thinkers—better people." Often, the only Internet stations in the school are in the library. Unlike other resources, students are not limited to an author's controlled choice of date—they are free to explore the world. Team planning and teaching with the resources begin with cooperatively planned school library activities for the students and shared in-services with evening instructors for the staff. Johnson suggests rubrics as foundational for both student technology development and teacher staff development. He articulates the clear roles of various school library personnel and wise budgeting based on the concept of "sustainable" technology.

I discovered that "information literacy" is a term that causes confusion (Linda Langford, 1998). School librarians themselves wonder if it is a reworking of an old term or a pedagogy unto itself. In the burgeoning of literature on the topic, one finds a myriad of definitions (Paul Richardson, 1996; Michael Eisenberg and Robert Berkowitz, 1990; ATLC, 1997). The Ontario School Library Association (1998) developed an information literacy curriculum for grades one through twelve based on their definition: "The ability to acquire, critically evaluate, select, use, create, and communicate information in ways that lead to knowledge and wisdom. It encompasses all other forms of literacy—traditional . . . media . . . numerical" (p. 2). The University of Calgary (1998), in its Library of the Future

Task Force, defines information literacy as "the broad information continuum which ranges from data to knowledge to wisdom . . . focuses on five broad abilities: to recognize the need for information, to know how to access information, to understand how to evaluate information, to know how to synthesize information, to be able to communicate information" (p. 2–3).

In developing information literacy, the educational model of resource-based learning might be unsettling for teachers, as it is open-ended and involves print, electronic, and human resources. Resource-based learning necessitates the collaborative planning role of the teacher-librarian actively engaging students in the learning process. It is not resource-based teaching, where a teacher has selected a variety of resources to complement a lesson. Instead, students direct their learning in stations or centers, building knowledge structures rather than receiving them as the teaching teams model, guide, and provide examples (Sykes, 1997). Resource collections themselves must be "accurate, current, take into consideration the varied interests, abilities, learning styles, special needs, and maturity levels of students. Further, they should have aesthetic, literary, or social value and be of quality physical format or technical design. They should present varying points of view and reflect the diversity of our society" (Calgary Board of Education, 1998, p. 2). In other words, schools must have sound collection-development policies so that when patrons demand to know "Why are you throwing away books?" standards and policies for intellectual freedom and quality learning resources are in place (Calgary Board of Education, 1998, Collection Development Plan, Regulation 3,012). Our students deserve the best, and in this information era, Patricia Manning (1997) reminds us that: ". . . Sound bytes of electronic information can be updated, downloaded, and read in a nanosecond. It behooves those of us who believe in the enormous power of the printed page to make sure the books we love—and hope to teach children to love—are attractive, readable, informative, and trustworthy" (p. 55).

No matter what the format—print or electronic—school librarians must engage students, teachers, and parents in the evaluation process. If teachers can conceptualize evaluation of learning resources within current learning theory, methodologies can be developed to pass these conceptualization processes to students. "Both methods and the learning resources used should consistently relay similar messages to the students . . . that thinking is valued, expected, required" (David Peat, Robert Mulcahy, Lorraine Wilgosh, 1997, p. 51). A key question for choosing exemplary materials is: "To what degree does the text encourage students to be involved in and take charge of their own learning?" (Peat, Mulcahy, Wilgosh, 1997)

Constructivist thought acknowledges that the solution is as important as the actual answer. As Robert Sylwester (1998) points out, teaching is a creative art with a scientific base. Sylwester urges teachers to familiarize themselves with new, dynamic brain research by educators and scientists. Educators must provide a "wide array of learning opportunities to engage students in experiencing, creating, and solving real problems using their own experiences and working with others" (Ann Leiberman, 1995).

Barbara Stripling (1997) states that school libraries and teacher-librarians must abandon former paradigms and accept the need to be involved in school reform, going beyond "structural changes to substantive changes in the culture of the school" (p. 89). The foundation of these school libraries will be to develop authentic learners that: construct or produce rather than reproduce meaning or knowledge; pursue disciplined inquiry; and find value in learning that goes beyond the school environment.

Material can be presented in a plethora of ways, and almost all work in the form of student projects in learning-rich environments is based on authentic assessment, authentic curriculum, professional development, and community participation.

The role of the professional in the school library is crucial to constructivist future school libraries. Linda Roberts (1996), director of the U.S. Department of Education's Office of Educational Technology, spoke about the role of the school library media specialist in many schools being one of leadership in a critical aspect: technology reform. What is really exciting to her is walking into a school and seeing that the school library is the center of information—not only information that resides in the library itself but also information resources that are located literally around the world. Roberts thinks that the role of the teacher-librarian as information specialist has not changed over time as much as it had evolved, enhanced by the tools of the information age and the resources that are now available to students and teachers in their classrooms. Because the school librarian has often been the early innovator of technology—the early user of technology—many now find themselves in the role of teacher mentor, computer trainer, and adviser!

Roberts says: "When I was a teacher, I'd ask the librarian to tell me about the really good books for my kids. I could always expect a helpful response. Today, teachers ask the librarian how to get online, how to link their students up to other classrooms and resources, and how to find the good resources that are there for students. I see that as an expansion of role rather than a change in role" (p. 15).

Paul Lupton (1997), from a study done in Australia, found that teacher-librarians have a dramatic effect on learners in situations of good practice with the curriculum role paramount. Where the teacher-librarian provides the information base, school library programs are models of technology in learning. Negative points from Lupton's research show that few teachers are aware of the potential of the teacher-librarian's role, and many see teacher-librarians as not working with them. Blanche Woolls (1997) writes about the teacher-librarian's leadership role as that of being active in restructuring, taking the lead in implementing site-based management, providing accurate technology information and advice, taking a leadership role in curriculum reform, alerting users to resources to support the curriculum, helping implement new methods to assess learning, having a clear media center vision to make teaching and learning more effective, providing timely professional information, and keeping stakeholders informed.

According to John Perry Barlow (Ron Chepesiuk, 1996), cofounder of the Electronic Frontier Foundation, it does not make sense for trees to die for the purpose of publishing and disseminating information. Barlow emplores all librarians to understand that what they do is create cognitive space in the environment, whether the library is in a school or public building or on a web site or something else. As Barlow states: "Librarians need to make sure that they provide a rich space where human beings can gather, interact, and become more than themselves. If librarians can do that, and do it well, they will be a part of the future. I know a lot of them are doing that right now" (p. 51).

TIP: Are there other experts in the field of school libraries or an aspect of school libraries that you are studying? What does the most current research say? Check out sources such as the Internet, school library periodicals, and recent publications. There is a wealth of literature and studies supporting school libraries to discover and share.

CHAPTER 4

The Journey: Establishing Goals, Outcomes, Plans

The next part of the journey began with a "mind map" that assisted me with bringing out the framework I needed to develop a triangulated model for an action research plan. I had been familiar with semantic maps and webs, using them regularly in various stages of student research projects in the school library. Using the technique myself to draw my ideas about the next plans of the research journey was very insightful. It let me focus more specifically on what the components of my study could be and who needed to be involved. From there, I designed a very messy-looking plan around which I could structure the exploration. Falling into place (below) was a triangulated approach to gathering data.

I formulated four key questions to serve as a framework of goals and outcomes for all of the stakeholders, students, and experts involved, using three major "events" or forums. The first question I created was to engage participants in describing the characteristics they perceived depicted an excellent school library of the twenty-first century. "Excellent" was deliberately chosen to push current learning paradigms and delve into the area of wise and leading-edge educational practice. This question was later ammended in some events to asking a subject to use "three main descriptors or adjectives," as participants tended to dwell on this question heavily.

The second focus question I wanted to ask was: "What is important about the relationship of school libraries to learning and teaching?" Outcomes here would, I hoped, lead to the area of information literacy and role of the teacher-librarian.

The third question I developed asked participants to describe impediments to equitable access to excellent school libraries for all students K–12. The question was tailored to: "Do you think that there might be impediments to equitable access to excellent school libraries for all students K–12? If so, describe them." Outcomes here would relate to factors that lead to the erosion of school libraries and cutbacks in personnel.

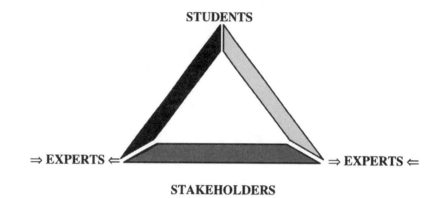

STUDENTS

⇒ EXPERTS ⇐   ⇒ EXPERTS ⇐

STAKEHOLDERS

Teacher-Librarians ◆ Library Staff ◆ Teachers ◆ Parents ◆ Leadership ◆ Community

The fourth question I needed to ask was for participants to consider how they might overcome some of these impediments. Here, outcomes sought needed to delve into the area of future recommendations for implementation and actions to be taken for transformation of future school libraries. It was hoped that not all of the outcomes arising would necessarily be tied to finances.

The first group of participants I worked with, identified as Event I, was individuals having association or university expertise in the field of school libraries. Seven individuals were identified from the literature search and invited, through e-mail, to participate in a telephone interview or to respond by e-mail. Participants were informed that their data would be shared with them for further input/editing.

The second group, Event II, was representatives from stakeholder groups within my large metropolitan school board. These representatives included teacher-librarians, library staff, teachers, parents, leadership figures, and community members. I sent an invitational questionnaire to them with an expected return date, noting that a focus group meeting would be arranged to bring them together to discuss the patterns and themes emerging from the questionnaire.

The third group, Event III, involved three student focus groups—elementary, junior high, and senior high—with whom I desired to tape-record group conversations. The logistics of doing this were complicated but solved by one group being led by a teacher-librarian I had trained and by receiving school-based permission for the second and third groups.

A fourth group, Event IV, enabled me to act as "participant-observer." This involved discussion and debate at meetings of the school library task force in my school board. The task force had 20 members representing a wide variety of stakeholders working to create a systemic vision for school libraries in our school board. To accomplish this, we brought our own "visions" to the group and shared them. A tool in use was the creation of a listserv (an e-mail discussion list) for us to post and debate "visions." A subcommittee was then selected to collaboratively write draft versions of a common vision. This enabled me to hear and reflect on 20 ideas of varying opinion on the future of school libraries while participating at the same time by sharing my hunch.

CHAPTER 5

Interventions: The Journey's Events

My journey continued with the implementation of the research—the "action events" planned. I wondered what responses I would get from my four questions and how they would inform the issue. What would I learn? What did this sampling of stakeholders think about school libraries?

Event 1: Expert Interviews

After going over my literature review and my involvement in the Association for Teacher-Librarianship in Canada (ATLC), I decided to contact "experts" in the field of school libraries via e-mail. I felt that the presidents of the Canadian and American national school library associations at the time would be wise choices to begin with, as they would have an overview and understanding of the present and future state of school libraries. I then sought representation from Canadian and American university experts, particularly those engaged in current research around school libraries. My university advisor and other educators also suggested "experts" to me.

In the e-mails, I identified myself as an M.Ed. student from the University of Portland doing an action research project on the future of school libraries. I added that the research project was grounded in the principles of the American Educational Research Association (AERA) and the American Psychology Association (APA), of which all of my university instructors were members. I mentioned that data collected would not be personalized but extrapolated from for analysis of patterns and themes and then shared with them. Six people readily agreed to participate in a telephone interview. What you will read next are the "voices" of the six experts—a part of my journey I found to be so rich.

➡️ **TIP:** Prior to conducting interviews, review materials and resources that discuss the successful conduction of an interview and be prepared to code the data.

I must admit I felt a little nervous as the clock ticked to the time that had been set up to interview my first expert in the field of school libraries: Dr. Dianne Oberg. At the time, Oberg headed the school library department at the University of Alberta, one of the few universities in Canada where teachers can do graduate work in school libraries. I had suggested that the telephone interview might take about 20 minutes, but almost an hour later, Oberg and I were still in discussion. Occasionally, I would jump in and contribute, finding that I had to stop myself from doing this so that I could hear the perspective of the expert. I had to remove myself from the role of collaborator to the role of interviewer.

Oberg very much feels that school libraries in the future need to build on what was excellent in the twentieth century: characteristics that included a schoolwide focus, a focus on teaching and learning, and providing an inviting environment. Oberg reminded me that teachers are our primary clientele. Thus, school libraries need to be staffed with teacher-librarians to provide teaching and learning support. Teacher-librarians need to be on the forefront of curriculum instruction, able to integrate Internet resources into instruction, and able to assist in the implementation of curriculum across the provinces.

Oberg feels that this support to teaching and learning goes far beyond curriculum into the teacher-librarian taking leadership in learning how to learn, in teaching the research process, and in using all kinds of materials in learning. Oberg's dream is that teaching and learning will become more fluid—more integrated into our daily lives. Not all learning materials need to be physically located in the library or school. Oberg also talked about other schools, such as info-centers and cyber schools. She has seen teacher-librarians working in information literacy in the community. In this "authentic pedagogy," learning would be of value outside of the school. She feels that assessing competence is the current focus, but we need to move out of the box regarding the way we think about teaching, learning, and school libraries. She thinks that excellent school library programs provide models for work outside of school. This "real world" work addresses the complex, unanswerable questions of learning rather than the dissemination of facts. But in this world outside the school, is there a guide on the way? Where do learners go for a guide? Taking leadership in developing authentic pedagogy is a role for the teacher-librarian.

Oberg feels that teachers and teacher-librarians need to be explicit about the research process and its importance to learning so that students can see patterns and connections, and so they can see that learning inside the school connects to learning outside. She gave examples from the world of work: Is this the type of research project a nurse would do in helping a patient? Is it the work someone at a telecommunications company would do to plan a new in-service? We need to plan, evaluate, and research for everyday lives—she feels that kids do not see the connection, and we do not help them to see it. This is the thing we call "lifelong learning," which is rooted in constructivism. Too often, we have decided the questions, the sources, etc., and this impedes our programs. We often have been the only audience for student work, but students need significant audiences. Oberg suggests that not every program in school needs to follow this model but that the school library program should adopt this focus on independent learning.

Another impediment to program development that Oberg discussed is that many teacher-librarians have seen the library as "my" program and services, not "ours"; to be successful, it must be a whole-school program. It is difficult to maintain authentic programs—to educate teachers about our role—but if we do, the demand will increase, not decrease. Right now, there are few qualified teacher-librarians in Alberta schools; teachers or other personnel are in charge of school libraries rather than those schooled in information. This arises from political emphasis on autonomy and site-based management. In general, Oberg believes that site-based management works, but in specific situations if it means schools have to make decisions in areas of little expertise, it is not a good use of site-based management. Few principals, teachers, or parents understand the value of an excellent school library program. They take what Oberg calls a "cardiac approach"—generally these people are very supportive, and they want and value a good school library, but their heart-felt approach doesn't mean they understand the complexity of resource-based learning. Even some teacher-librarians do not understand the complexities. Even though research, such as the "Colorado Study," shows how good libraries and staffs improve student learning, individual teacher-librarians must become aware of the research and work with their principals and parents. Oberg likened this to a "novice" and "expert" view of the world, again using the metaphor of a nurse. Some might see a nurse tucking a patient into bed and think that is all they do, but, in reality, they also make critical observations about the patient. Dr. Oberg is concerned about the inequity across the province and that "have-not" schools are increasing in number. The impact is not easy to measure in the short term.

Oberg offered many ideas for how to overcome some of the impediments. If novice and experienced teacher-librarians have a supportive network of other teacher-librarians, they will develop more capacity to demonstrate good practice themselves, and they will share ideas for developing support. District policy must support principals who support teacher-librarians. Policies must also support and enable change. So many good programs disappear when a "good" principal or teacher-librarian leaves. (Oberg is disheartened that she has observed these cases where years of work were "dashed," and it was hard for people to start again because they felt they had failed.) Professional associations could lobby at the ministry level and work with other associations involving parents, teachers, and principals. Not only are few new teacher-librarians being hired but few new teachers are as well. Oberg knows that learning to be a teacher-librarian is harder than learning to be a teacher because there are fewer models.

Oberg discussed with me the area of teacher education at the University of Alberta as becoming much broader and taking on the attitude of "a whole school (village) being needed to educate a child." In fact, their student teachers are now sent out in teams or cohorts to learn to work together using collaborative methods and are not expected to be the "master of the class." The university's teacher-librarian program focuses on teaching research from a constructivist base and on learning to address the demands of educational change. Having the distance-learning program for teacher-librarians on the Internet will make a twofold difference: Students will be using technology and learning how to implement it at the same time. These programs of teacher and teacher-librarian education reflect a break from the norms of the closed classroom. We still have a lot of closed classrooms and teachers who would find it difficult to talk about teaching practice—their own or someone else's. Unless teachers and teacher-librarians are able to talk about their teaching practice, it is very difficult to improve teaching and learning for students.

My next interview was with Pat Taylor, president of the Association for Teacher-Librarianship in Canada at the time (October 1997). Taylor had prepared at length to participate. Although I was the editor of the association's journal, *Impact*, I had not had an opportunity to meet Taylor and was delighted to "meet" her through an inspiring conversation.

Taylor began the interview by commenting that, as Yogi Berra once said: "Prediction is very hard—especially when it's about the future." She discussed societal trends at length, reinforcing their importance to keep in mind for this work. In the industrial society, education was separated from society. She stated that we can no longer afford that separation. With population growth in Canada at approximately 1.7 births per family, a high percentage of the country's growth will come from immigration. As we look to characterize the school library of the future, we have to ask: "What immigration? Where are families coming from? What is their cultural background?" In some provinces, like Saskatchewan and Alberta, the student populace might look different than in British Columbia or Ontario. In places like Saskatchewan, the native population is increasing. Government resource allocations will shift toward an aging population. How can libraries be designed from an income base of people who do not have children directly involved in schools? How do we involve them? Taylor talked about the competing market-place; independent schools, home-schooling, and different styles of education and wondered: Who do we need to involve in our marketing? She also spoke about a significant increase of children with special needs, such as autism, fetal alcohol syndrome, brain injury, and cognitive delays resulting from premature birth. This creates a profound effect on students who come to us and their parents' expectations, leading to broader issues of school expectations—the search for definable standards and the idea from corporate America that education "train" for employment, rather than educate. School libraries with their problem-solving continuums might not be as valued as those things that can be measured with economic value demanded.

Taylor also said that school libraries of the future must go beyond the idea of being "research facilities"; many educators, including school librarians, have not adjusted to the new realities of libraries in the "post-modem school" as information centers. Teacher-librarians must become information managers—using the term "information" in its broadest application—to go far beyond physical access to resources into intellectual access to resources. This access is not equitable across the formats of media; some, such as certain Internet sites, get us to the point of access, but what value do they have? There is little student mediation for the Internet or multi-channel television, which creates a new societal culture. Taylor likened the Internet to a classroom with 100,000 television channels with most of the content being advertising; we show students how to access information but do not teach them the skills for mediating that information. The school library can be a place for shared culture—we used to be able to converse about the one television channel we watched—so how can we move students to some sort of shared experience and understanding with the 100,000?

Taylor stated that we need to get serious about what we mean in regard to information literacy. There is a change of roles and responsibilities for students and educators as well as a change in relationships. Taylor noted that Alan November talks about the vast difference between "informating" and "automating." Teachers are in the business of informating: facilitating learning so that students can become informed citizens. School libraries are busy getting automated. Taylor believes that you can automate all you want, but you might end up with nothing more than a $2,000 pencil. If we're not informating, there is little value for the dollar. For example, Taylor read about an e-mail correspondence project involving American and Middle East students. "Virtual" conflict occurred on the topic of religion because the Middle East students spelled "God" without an "o." Spelling the word in full was, in their set of beliefs, disrespectful, whereas for the students from the southern states, spelling God's name in full was a sign of respect. The students of both cultures became angry, thinking each was being disrespectful. The relationship on e-mail had to go deeper than "how is the climate, food, etc., different in your country?" In Canada, we might have students from one province in virtual projects with students from a province that does not believe in separatism.

Although educators, including teacher-librarians, know about the many ways of learning, Taylor wonders if we honor these ways, if we "walk the talk." She went on to say that we do not read the same way from a screen that we do from a book. Media instruction is like second-language instruction. We take the theory and define it, but do we have things other than books in the library? Do we teach students to search for materials, and then leave them without looking after the metacognitive? Taylor spoke about Toffler's prediction that the illiterate of the future will not be those that cannot read and write but those who cannot unlearn and relearn. Formulas such as the "Big 6" steps to research (Eisenberg and Berkowitz, 1990) will not be as succinct in a world where students need to make order out of chaos.

Taylor talked about the consequences of technology "biting back at us"; about the unanticipated results of technology. An example of this in her district involved using e-mail for interlibrary loans. They had to increase trucks, mail days, etc., as 25,000 e-mails per year for sharing of materials ensued! Teacher-librarians need to look at the teacher's role of providing equity of access to the school library or not; after all, it is the teacher who decides whether it is to be "the book" used in the classroom and nothing else. Some teachers will not learn about resource-based learning and will continue the patterns of the way they did things. This excludes equity. If we teach and learn within our own comforts, we ignore others' learning styles. On some schedules, students are taken to the library for half an hour a week, whether they need to go or not. Would teachers benefit if they were "made to go"? If educators are not learners and continuous learners, we are impediments to equity.

Taylor mentioned the "Kellogg Report" (1996), a study done through the Benton Foundation in the United States on how library leaders see the future of libraries and how the public sees it. Librarians pictured hybrid institutions with librarian navigators. The public was not sure if libraries should be this kind of electronic hub but rather on the margin—doing readings, etc. Families with children loved libraries. Other members of the public saw libraries as democratic institutions providing the "have-nots" of the future with information. All agreed that libraries needed to transform from being collectors and disseminators to being information creators. Taylor thinks school librarians spend little time in the outer edge of being creators.

Taylor feels that partnerships are a powerful way of educating people for the libraries of the future. We have to overcome our own paradigm of control and develop curious, questioning people. We should not add on to what we already have, then look and talk the same. As school librarians, we have to step away from what we have, then take out and replace our own thinking—free ourselves from impediments of what we know, then go back to what we know. Unfortunately, we have not given our teachers the time, professional development, or university education to make this shift.

Next, in October 1997, I spoke with Barbara Stripling, the then president of the American Association of School Libraries (AASL). For the third time, it seemed as though "like minds" had connected, no matter how many miles apart, allowing us to engage in collegial dialogue that school librarians rarely get to do when holding that one unique position on a staff. Stripling began by reinforcing that students and their learning must be the focus of the future rather than "school libraries"; that the school library of the future be a seamless part of the school with in-depth, inquiry-based learning using authentic assessment practices. School libraries in the future must make connections to the real world, with students being responsible for their own learning. I really liked the way she went on to define information literacy as "process" or "learning how to learn." This mirrors the way I feel about action research. Stripling and I discussed that action research would be a good model for student research.

She added that many teachers require content; in the school library, we strive to teach process. Teacher-librarians must become a part of every classroom experience with collaborative planning and teaching. Stripling made an interesting distinction between the "cooperative planning" teacher-librarians were using and "collaborative planning," a higher level of cooperative planning that is more challenging and rewarding. There is reluctance on the part of teachers to accept teacher-librarians as equals; this is partly their fault if they are focused on just the library. If they are focused on the curricular topic, such as World War II, they can offer our expertise in the planning meeting. If teachers get as much as they give in the process, they will buy in if they see the resources as "ours," not the librarians.

Stripling went on to say that, in the twenty-first century, school libraries will provide points of connection for students to the outside world—between subjects—allowing the world to come in and connect to their lives. Her ultimate goal is that future school libraries become community centers of learning as the point of connection between the local community and the school. These centers would have parent resources, involve businesses, and use real-world information and activities on topics such as: income taxes, banking, family literacy, family learning experiences, storytelling festivals, and older people reading to youth. These school libraries must have production capabilities, as students not only need to know but "to do" in all different formats in any number of ways. Stripling has struggled with the idea of the library as a physical place and has concluded that it must be a physical place, as she feels we cannot live without books. But it could be more than a physical place if the role of the teacher-librarian was that of conceptual organizer of information processes into classrooms and the community.

Stripling spoke about a seamless integration of resources and teaching around the essence of a topic—depth on topics is not often found in textbooks that are geared for coverage. School libraries must build collections that support inquiry—where students can dig in and learn on their own. This cannot happen unless you organize by higher concepts and have resources to help students build knowledge. Students do need facts, but they also need opportunities to put the facts into construction and work together to solve problems. Students need to formulate their own questions. Library projects give students these opportunities and lend themselves to group work. This group work needs to be complex, using facts to solve a problem together.

Stripling stated the importance of students learning from reflection, which can easily be built into library work. For example, designing reflection points after every step or so in research projects. This "recursive," nonlinear learning—with time for reflection—gives students permission to say "No, I'm not where I want to be" and follow their own mental processes. So much of a library is independent work, giving time and incentive to reflect. It cannot have "locked steps." Stripling shared a good idea for designing notetaking for reflection: on the left side of a page, write the facts; on the right side, describe reflections about those facts or discoveries.

Stripling noted the need for educators to offer both support and challenge to student learning. It was a long process she went through to come to this; to go beyond saying "good job." We do not reach our highest levels unless someone challenges us. School librarians must ask hard questions of students. Within the library environment, students can learn about diverse viewpoints and dealing with those in our age of information. They can learn to sift through and select the best information, then draw conclusions. Libraries need to be a source of complexity in learning. So many learning activities are pre-organized with one viewpoint. Someone else has done the thinking for students to absorb and "spit back." This does not reflect the world that the students will live in! They need to hone these skills to cope in a protective and supportive environment with carefully selected resources.

Stripling feels that impediments to equity for excellent school library programs are part of a broadening gap of money for resources and technology. In some schools, parents fill in the gap, but in others, they cannot. We do not have enough data on the effects of school libraries on achievement. Another big impediment is non-flexible scheduling. With flexible scheduling of the librarian, the library can become a learning center open to students at all times. Another impediment is that, unfortunately, many teacher-librarians are without vision or access to professional development in a field where not only pedagogy but content can change daily, unlike some of the subject teachers. Lack of active administrative support from the governments can be disempowering. Leaders must lead the way to inquiry learning; you need a climate of inquiry in the school to have an inquiry library. With librarians often being at the center of technological change, lack of technical support can also be an impediment.

What needs to be done? Stripling feels that resource learning needs to be a part of every graduate and undergraduate education degree. Teachers themselves must experience learning in the way we want them to teach. Teacher-librarians need their own staff development as well as a real focus on education issues to expand our definition of "library" into being the instructional leader in the school. Teacher-librarians need to learn how to help people understand what a library can do for students, communities, and schools.

Ensuing interviews were briefer, perhaps because I was getting better at interviewing and zeroing in on certain points or patterns! I next interviewed University of Portland professional librarian Pam Horan (October 1997). Horan thinks that excellent future school libraries are going to be a variety of things. First, she feels that libraries should provide basic resource support for students plus the broader range of audio-visual materials and links to the outside world with the Internet and other technologies we might not yet know about. Technologies change rapidly with items such as typing online, class sessions linked to classrooms in different parts of the world, interactive talking, and distance education courseware. Students from New York could share opinions and pictures with students in Oregon, working on group projects together. The school library would take a lead role in making these links.

Horan also said that school libraries of the future should be about "give-and-take learning": Educators feed children's curiosity and sense of discovery with resources and communications they provide. The independence of students should be encouraged in their searching and sense of discovery in pursuing their own interests. Students of all ages (including graduate students) will gain a sense of mastery and success in doing this. Horan gave an example of her niece doing a report on Andy Warhol, using various sources. Her niece was excited about what she found during her search. Libraries support that excitement. Impediments to all students having these experiences are structural in the way the educational system is set up and how schools are financed locally. For geographic or demographic reasons, many homes are without cultural enrichment to spark that excitement about learning. If students cannot read, how can they use or feel comfortable with libraries? Volunteering might give opportunity to parents to learn about the library.

Horan observed that new technologies take a long time to teach and are labor intensive with more one-on-one or small-group teaching. New technology requires staff development for the librarian, teachers, and students to use it or fix it because technical support is badly underfunded.

Horan thinks that a way to overcome some of the impediments is through collaboration and partnerships between schools and public libraries. More collaboration between teachers and teacher-librarians is essential, while some librarians find this "hard to do." Horan and I agreed that this does take a lot of energy and can be met with resistance on the part of the instructors. Horan thinks that some librarians might be introverted and not feel as confident in these collaborations, especially with the new technologies. They need to develop skills to communicate with the faculty, even if they know how to communicate with the students. Before we purchase more technology, we need to ask these questions: Why do we want it? How will we support it? What outcomes do we seek?

I next conducted an interview (November 1997) with an internationally known figure in school librarianship: Ken Haycock, a former president of the Canadian Library Association, the Canadian School Library Association, the American Association of School Libraries, and publisher of *Teacher-Librarian*. Haycock is well placed to consider the future of school libraries as a former school principal, senior education official, and elected school board chair. He is currently director of the Graduate School of Library, Archival and Information Studies at the University of British Columbia.

Haycock thinks that school libraries of the future might look different to some extent but that the functions will not change too much. He feels strongly that clear statements need to come from the district as to what purpose school libraries should serve. When I asked him what he thought that purpose might be, he replied: "To enable students to access and make effective use of information and ideas in all forms and formats." With the trend for districts to have site-based decision-making, many library programs erode at the same time that information explodes. He also emphasized the necessity to build partnerships with communities and the public library as other information providers. He sees a societal move to connecting learning communities with schools as one player.

Haycock thinks that the role of the teacher-librarian will not be that different—that of having expertise in useful sources of information and how young people learn. It makes sense to have one qualified person managing the library to avoid duplication of efforts. Teachers do not have that level of competence or cannot do it alone. The school library must build into classroom programs. Haycock feels there is ample evidence in research studies that demonstrates having a teacher-librarian adds to reading motivation, achievement, and information literacy. He thinks that many teacher-librarians are not aware of these studies. They tie themselves to their own advocacy rather than advocacy for the students. He commented on the poor education of most teacher-librarians in the sense that he often hears about teachers being put in charge of libraries or used as "relief" teachers without having diplomas or master's degrees in the field. Haycock also commented that teacher-librarians must focus on professional duties, not clerical ones. He does see the role of the teacher-librarian as becoming more important in areas such as finding web sites and bookmarking them, using search engines, using the Internet and establishing Internet ethics so that we do not require filters, and fitting resources together as a whole.

Haycock mentioned Library Power as a success in the United States. Private funding and a sound evaluation plan made for an interesting example of funding granted because of demonstrated achievement. The Los Angeles school board puts in more money to libraries than other states due to this coordinated national advocacy plan, which Canada does not as yet have but hopes will emerge from the national symposium in 1997. Haycock hopes that this symposium will lead to something like the American Library Association's 1988 Library Power.

Haycock concluded by giving me another contact: Pat Cavill, a private library marketing consultant hired by the publishing industry to study why youth book sales are declining. Her study earmarked the erosion of collections and professionals in school libraries as major factors affecting the youth publishing industry (Cavill, 1997). Haycock also informed me about another school library task force in his province and suggested I contact them about getting a copy of the results. I did not meet with success in having that board share its conclusions.

The final "expert" interview for this part of my journey was with Dr. Joy McGregor (November 1997). McGregor was then an assistant professor (now an associate professor) at the School of Library and Information Studies at Texas Woman's University. I discovered that McGregor had taken courses with Dr. Oberg at the University of Alberta in 1978. A small world! McGregor also was developing a research study that would use the interview process to gather data and was curious to experience the interviewee's perspective. Although she felt that excellent school libraries were somewhat dependent on the district or governmental climate, she strongly stated that excellent school libraries need to be learning centers and extensions of the classroom. Traditionally, students have learned in the classroom, gotten "stuff" from the library, and gone back and learned in the classroom. In a group of high school students that McGregor had recently spent some time with, the students were still in that paradigm and did not see research as involving the thought process. One student, even though he had taken extensive notes from a source in the library, remarked that he felt "brain-dead that day, and all I did was collect information concerning the topic." He did not say anything about reading it. Students need to make the vital connection with research as a learning process—an integral part of learning, not a "frill" or "add on" to the day.

McGregor mentioned, as the others had, that the school library of the future should be part of the larger community—both physically and virtually—noting that there are a lot of other libraries. Referencing the SCANS report, the jobs our students will go into in the future will be so foreign from schools that even computer labs will look like "junk" to some students who have superior technologies at home. School libraries need to be on the cutting edge of technology, not just up-to-date. Adjectives she used to sum up this place were "vibrant, active, ever-changing with curriculum and learning theory, responsive, networked, involved."

McGregor reminded me that the information specialist or teacher-librarian in these "information centers" provides the connections among ideas because information does not always fit into "neat little packages." The information center provides the nonsynthesized information and the teacher-librarian helps students see the connections among the ideas. Teacher-librarians must see the bigger "package"—more so than the classroom teacher—and promote interdisciplinary curricula. Teacher-librarians can also follow student growth over a number of years and might see where a student has grown or where he or she needs guidance that the classroom teacher is not yet aware of. Resource-based learning leads to critical thinking and the evaluation of the information that is so crucial in a democratic, noncensored society. The school library is a natural catalyst for collaborative processes involving students, parents, teachers, and administrators.

McGregor thinks that the largest impediment to this active learning center is "status quo"—continuing on as we always have is just easier. In fact, in a district in Texas where 23 out of 24 elementary schools went to flexible library scheduling, the lone holdout was recognized as a "Blue Ribbon School"—an initiative of the U.S. Department of Education. McGregor will investigate this further.

McGregor believes that too many stakeholders involved do not understand the role or potential of the school library, including many teacher-librarians themselves. Sometimes, this negative influence can seem stronger than the positive. For teacher-librarians, communication to the stakeholders is critical, but this communication must reflect the importance to learning—not only items such as how much you made at the book fair, but also: "How can I make a difference in your classroom?" Stakeholders must see what is in it for them, which McGregor referred to as educating others either formally or informally. She also mentioned that national or local standards need to be set: In Texas, whole schools—including their libraries—are evaluated on a grid. As for funding? Parents are tired of the constant need to raise funds. Schools must seek active partnerships with businesses, and teacher-librarians, especially in the United States, need to be aggressive about seeking grants.

Event 2: Calgary Board of Education Stakeholders

The second tool I explored in the triangulated approach was sampling written responses to my research questions from two representatives of my school board stakeholder groups, followed by a focus group meeting. The focus group met over coffee and dessert to discuss emerging patterns and themes from this research. The representation included two teacher-librarians from each level: elementary, junior high, and senior high; three senior district administrators; two parents; two library technicians; two school-based administrators; and my team partner, also a teacher-librarian. Of the 16 invited, 12 were returned. Based on another hunch that is developing on this journey, I will need stronger representation from classroom teachers in focus groups. I had thought that was somewhat covered because teacher-librarians and others were classroom teachers at one time, but perspectives vary as roles change.

The first thing that both surprised and delighted me was the congruence of the themes and patterns that emerged from the expert interviews and literature. The school library in the future must be the brightest, most welcoming place in the school, with much student work displayed and parents coming in regularly to see this. Full-time "library staff with appropriate training" was mentioned throughout the contributions, with a suggestion about taking the teacher-librarian out of the pupil-teacher ratio. School libraries without librarians cannot be used in the manner that ones with librarians can. Equity of access to current information in all formats for all students was critical and possible with full-time, appropriately qualified staff. Where this was not possible, shared staffing agreements could be a desirable alternative and work-experience students could benefit.

Teacher-librarians must be learning leaders, teaching partners, and resource experts that facilitate learning cultures across curriculums in schools. Schools need this learning and teaching leader, and if the librarian does not evolve into this role, the library might have a technician as the only adult, full-time resident. The teacher-librarian position must be understood and valued. The school library cannot be the domain of one person. All staff must feel that they have been a part of shaping the change to an inviting, non-threatening environment—a place for "love, adventure, fantasy"! Children and young adults can reflect upon their lives and the roles that they might take on. This leadership extends into fully automated libraries, with technology integration in multimedia literacy and telecommunications, such as interactive video, satellites, smart boards, and electronic databases, predominating in the nonfiction area. The teacher-librarian will be the ultimate human "interface" for the technology and the students, providing the students with strategies of information management and sharing human concerns in a real-time, global, fast-paced world.

Site-based decision-making needs to be informed with predetermined school library policies and guidelines. Many uninformed stakeholders still do not recognize the importance of information literacy for the twenty-first century, with much time wasted on the need to "convince" decision-makers about this importance. An aging teaching population that has barely changed practice over time leads to lack of continuity of program as students move from grade to grade or school to school. Do we ignore or "work around" these individuals? If we move from standard textbook-driven curriculums to exploratory learning that uses textbooks only as a starting point, school libraries will be an essential part of student learning. Students need to be taught how to learn and to learn how to find what they need to know. According to educational directives we should be pursuing, the individual of the future will be a questioner, risk taker, creator, and innovator. Without quality school library programs, this might never occur.

School libraries should have a regional as well as global focus. Quality fiction and nonfiction written by members of minority communities should be included. There should be some allowance for leisure books students enjoy, such as comics or series. Staff and students will both be required to develop critical thinking, analytic skills to use, access, and evaluate data. This learning needs to be activated and used in presentations demonstrating construction of knowledge. As content areas change so fast, students will need tools to access them as they change. Access cannot be restricted to the privileged; there must be an understanding that libraries can play a vital role in delivering equity of access. Using local and wide-range networks would lead to more virtual access as well as connections from the school library to classrooms, homes, and other libraries at all hours to provide real-time opportunities for the whole community. Those skilled in information science can make sure students receive the most they can from the worldwide network we call the Internet, facilitating effective decision-making based on time constraints and volumes of information. Guidance will be needed on issues of copyright and plagiarism.

It is imperative to create a supportive, meaningful environment for engaged, effective learning linked to curriculum. The school library should be the hub or focal point of the school. Library materials can make teaching more meaningful and interesting, allowing real research that works to solve problems such as environmental, communication, safety, security, governance, violence, and tolerance issues. Students need to be directed toward independent learning, broadening their knowledge to form their own opinions or conclusions that have been well thought out and researched by being exposed to a range of ideas and viewpoints and reading for enjoyment. Literature must be celebrated. Students with exceptional learning or language needs and different learning styles will need adaptive methodologies that school libraries can accommodate.

Inadequate and inequitable funding was seen as an impediment for both new and older schools. Collections need to be of the best quality and up-to-date with materials in all formats integrated on the shelves so that users can see at a glance where everything is located. The school library needs a revamping of the look and atmosphere. The old notion of libraries as stagnant places where one should be quiet transforms into a light, "airy," wide-open space filled with students at discussion tables instead of "dusty, crowded shelves; dark smelly corners; old, fading posters." If school libraries cling to a model of the past, the rest of the school might move on, and the library will become an anomaly and wither. Print material is still a priority, especially where it might be superior to digital. District and system support are important to solving the equity issue through such services as evaluating resources, allowing small-budget schools the ability to share resources, centrally purchasing expensive resources, and including staff development opportunities. The National Symposium on Information Literacy in Ottawa, which occurred November 19–22, 1997, took place in light of the need for consistent national standards. It was thought that recommended guidelines commit schools to maintain programs and resources that are not sacrificed due to an individual's personality or conflict of values.

Event 3: Calgary Board of Education Students

The third event of this process was initially difficult to arrange but ultimately rewarding—the voice of our students through three focus groups. First of all, I was unable to visit an elementary school, but a colleague I knew agreed to interview a group of fifth- and sixth-graders. He tried to simplify the research questions for them, but they still found it a hard exercise to look at the future. They were very happy with their current exemplary media center. They did wish that technology allowed better searching capabilities with more description of what you would find once you got there. Computers should be multifunctional, faster, and in "words kids can understand." They spoke about a need for more audio-visual resources, including maps. These students believed in constructing knowledge;

they liked choosing their own topics and using a variety of resources—books, videos, software, Internet. They spoke about the need for lots of access—at some schools they had been in, you could only go to the library once a week, and there were poor resources. This did not work well because you could be waiting several days to get new books or information on something that you really wanted to learn about. Besides more money, these students felt schools could share resources more, as long as the students took care of them.

Secondly, I was able to visit a junior high school and conduct a tape-recorded interview with a group of seventh-, eighth-, and ninth-graders. From this session, I was able to discern common points. The students were excited about talking to me and were full of ideas. It was so energizing! Unanimously, the students felt that the school library in the future had to be "high-tech"—technology in the name of computers needed to be accessible in the school library. But some of them went on to describe electronic organizers, books on discs with 3-D graphics, and virtual reality stations—if one was studying the middle ages, one would put on a glove and do battle in a virtual world! They wished that the library did not have restricted access and that they could access it from home or come into the school library in the evening and work. They felt parents or their teachers might volunteer to supervise these extra hours. They all spoke strongly about wanting the school library to have more of a community focus. This stemmed from some practical concerns, such as parents having to drive them to the public library. Some students were aware that libraries, such as The Library of Congress, were open 24 hours a day online.

They wished that school libraries permeated a sense of greater trust and worried about the newly installed electric gates, lack of space for their backpacks, and traditional insistence on quiet. They wanted the library to be comfortable. They realized the realm of student responsibility needed to help care for the library and came up with the idea of a student library upgrading club. They spoke about their own learning styles as being diverse—some needed noise or music to work in; others needed visuals; others needed quiet areas, such as study carrels with computers. One of the ninth-graders commented that certain technologies might be helpful to some peers he knew of that could not read well.

Materials need to be up-to-date and relevant. The students expressed the need for books reflecting "pop culture," as they are often asked in social studies or language arts to do projects in current events. They spoke about the need for weeding—getting rid of old books that were literally falling apart—and getting current books on topics they needed for school assignments. They worried about not having enough Canadian materials. The students got into a lively discussion regarding the future of books, with many feeling that books worked the imagination in a different way than computers. One student presented me with his "Library of the Future" wish list that he had prepared on an index card:

- more computers
- scanner
- better printer
- Digi-Pad (to draw)
- a real card catalog
- virtual glove
- reading carousel
- comfortable chairs
- more sci-fi
- more Jane Goodall
- microfiche reader (for old newspapers)
- easier to see (open spaces)
- knapsack section
- sound-field barrier
- intelligence computer
- voice command
- fax machine (Internet fax from the Library of Congress)
- CNN hookup
- working water fountain
- Albert Einstein's Theory of Relativity book

The teacher-librarian had to leave the group to teach a class for a short time and was so enthused with the discussion that she carried it on in her seventh-grade language arts class. She then presented me with some of their responses. The seventh-graders expressed similar ideas to the previous group, with a few interesting digressions. Fiction would transmit to your home computer via open links, eliminating lost or late books. Big screens would show "pre-taped reports, teachers who are sick, principal or emergency messages." Would pets be allowed and would there be such a thing as "educational Nintendo"? Books would fall into "luggage carriers" when you ordered them from computers. One student wrote: "They will actually have good books," which I thought was kind of a sad reflection on what I have observed in many dated, unweeded collections. Computers on the sides of bookshelves might tell about what is on that shelf. Unlike current trends for smaller school library spaces, students unanimously requested larger, more colorful school libraries with one student taking it to the extreme of elevators and large screens in different rooms. You might see authors writing books there or have a "meet your favorite author" station. Have we considered a machine like a pop machine that gives books? And would those be "floppy" books? A few students liked the way school libraries were today—just add more books and computers.

Thirdly, there was a senior high school group. A couple of the students sent essays on the topic—with one individual sending a tape—prior to my visit. Meeting the students over lunch was again energizing. There was another clear message about having access to technology with user-friendly systems. One student thought virtual reality would be of interest, with books on CD ready to be downloaded— perhaps for a fee. Other students saw the computer as a tool and articulated strongly for books. They thought the purpose of a library was about reading. They spoke about their love of books, how you could "take a book to bed with you," and how they thought paper books would always be around. What types of books? Romance (especially historical), science fiction, and fantasy. They thought current information, periodicals, and encyclopedias—but not fiction—should be electronic. All formats of materials were important to everyone's different learning styles. The school library should provide objective materials on sensitive topics. Students felt they needed information on subjects where they might feel confused, such as homosexuality.

The environment needs to be conducive to learning, with enough room for "several people to put their books and binders on the table." Once again, the students talked about trust—they did not like the "censor gates" and backpack checks or adults hovering around them, suspicious about every move. They tentatively broached the subject of staff and heartily recommended teacher-librarians. The "teacher" part of that gave them a person who understood students, their learning, and their curriculum. One student commented that he would like to see two or three teacher-librarians able to assist students with more in-depth research work. Students wished they could do in-depth research on their own topics. Students felt they needed a place to study—where a knowledgeable staff should be available to help them. School libraries in the future should have "good resources"— a wide range of current (every year or two), accurate materials that match the curriculum was necessary. Increasing numbers was not enough though; finding the article was part of the problem. Sometimes, libraries provide more opportunities for student learning than they are currently receiving in the classroom.

Money was thought to be a major impediment to school libraries, with the suggested solution of a greater affiliation with the community, including partnerships between schools and other institutions to make the most of limited resources and needless redundancy. Students suggested selling old materials to buy new ones. As knowledge increases, students felt access was decreasing for commonly needed sources, such as encyclopedias and Internet access becoming "overstrained." Materials bought even five years ago are "used, abused, and outdated," thus the standard of learning obtained five years ago is no longer available due to degradation. Using these resources on a "first come, first serve" basis limited their research. They suggested extending library hours and perhaps charging user fees so that the community could use the library in the evenings.

The student focus groups seemed to have a great deal of concern with "access," which I got the impression was in the physical sense of checking out materials. Few of them, as McGregor pointed out in her interview, seemed to be getting onto the purpose of access to use: making connections and understandings.

This, I believe, is a reflection on how resource-based learning had been implemented (or not) within the educational experience of these particular students. Perhaps their classrooms had not been involved in inquiry, information literacy projects, cooperative learning, and so forth, in school library experiences.

Shortly after interviewing the student groups, I was fortunate to receive a small action research grant from my school board. This grant enabled me to cooperatively plan a student focus group day with the three volunteer teacher-librarians I had been working with. The fund provided substitute coverage for the teacher-librarians as well as for supplies for the students. The three teacher-librarians held a number of virtual (e-mail, phone, fax) planning sessions, then spent one of the covered afternoons planning in real time. What a powerful afternoon for all—four teacher-librarians collaboratively planning together! The ensuing plan focused around four issues for the students to work through: What do you most enjoy in your school library? What type of assignments/projects/activities do you do in your school library now? What would you like to do? What about the year 2005? We debated about putting a date on the future but agreed that the students could put it in a framework of their future high school or family.

The actual day arrived with 18 students attending, ranging from grades five through twelve. It was a resounding success for all participants in the sense of the intensity of the work and the learning we did from each other. One of the teacher-librarians, adept with technology, prepared a draft video of the day, incorporating the photos, live action, and headings. Student evaluations of the day brought forward an element we had not anticipated: Nearly every one of the students commented on how much they enjoyed working with the different age groups as a primary benefit of the day! We noticed that it was very collaborative; the senior high students whom we thought might lead the groups—and did at some points—nevertheless shared the leadership, reporting, and other roles equally with the other ages. It was great that the students themselves made this reflection. The students left with science-fiction stories to complete. Three groups completed their stories. They hope to share them on the web.

As the stories started arriving, I noticed a much "darker" feel from the secondary group; a feel that they are being controlled and that the library in the future will be something like an Orwellian 1984, with characters such as evil cyborgs. This might be due to adolescent angst, sci-fi books or movies, or educational experiences that have not been student-centered or student-directed.

Event 4: Calgary Board of Education Library Task Force

As participant-observer in Event 4, I began to reflect that traditional meetings were not going to move the work forward. Everyone had an opinion and wished to voice it around the table. In consultation with technical services, we created a school library task force listserv. To do this, technical services required a charter, mandate, and rules for posting. The rules actually worked well as a mechanism for keeping individuals focused on our primary goal—student learning—and leaning away from day-to-day operations. It initially gave each of the 20 stakeholder representatives a forum for expression. This produced a vast amount of rich data, which was synthesized into a chart. The purpose of the chart was to integrate the listserv patterns with the student focus group patterns, particularly adding a section on the role of the teacher-librarian.

From all of these patterns and themes, I attempted to write a draft vision for future school libraries. An interactive session was held where the task force responded to this draft. A rich session evolved—think of a system task force editing your writing attempt! I learned so much from their comments and discussion; I found my thinking processes pushed ahead—"out of the box." A suggestion arose that four volunteers and I form a writing subcommittee to work on the draft, post it on the listserv, and prepare for further editorial sessions.

CHAPTER 6

Results and Discussions: Patterns, Themes, Conclusions

As one becomes involved in the processes of action research, one seems to become immersed in them and they "snowball." Indeed, some conclusions were drawn from this work at this point, but through the process, I do feel like this journey has a myriad of beginnings, not endings. It has enabled me to understand the mission; in this case, librarians as "archivists" of knowledge and teachers as "nurturers" of knowledge—therefore, teacher-librarians as both, which is why we are what we are rather than "media" or "information" specialists. From a mission, vision ensues. And through the processes of action research, this vision transforms into action, which leads to deep reflection. Action research is constructivist in the truest sense—one gains wisdom through seeing patterns, systems, strategies, and networks when working through issues or events with others.

Throughout the process, five patterns or themes were identified. One pattern that arose from most stakeholders, regardless of age or role, was the need for schools and school libraries of the future to actively comprehend and implement learning founded on constructivist theory. Information literacy is an outcome of these opportunities for learners to put facts into construction, to work together to solve problems, and to create. Curriculum moves from the need of "covering it" to "uncovering" it, as underlying structures and constructs emerge for rich learner connections. As learning becomes student-directed rather than teacher-directed, future libraries will transform from collecting and accessing resources to places of information creation. School libraries can take the lead in working through the develop- mental perspective of curriculum from key concepts to conceptual systems to disciplinary theories to interdisciplinary connections as conceptualized on the following chart.

MOVING TOWARD
CONSTRUCTIVIST SYSTEMS

Concept of Knowledge: Curriculum:	Instruction:		Learning:	
	Teacher/Teacher-Librarian Roles		*Learner Roles*	
Transformation Theory	*Guide*	*Frustration*	Inquiry	
Content-Learner	*Mentor*	*Error*	Generative	
Constructs	*Facilitator*	*Explorer*	Clear Object	
Developmental	*Critical Friend*	*Discoverer*	Resource-Based	
Systems	*Work With*	*Active*	Projects	
Problems	*Open Questions*	*Reason*	Interdisciplinary	
Knowledge Within Learner	*Collaborative*	*Engaged*	Comparative	
"Seeing" the Learner	*Researcher*	*Whole*		
Constructivist	*Teams*	*Self-Reliant*	Wisdom	
		Co-operative	Connected	
		Ownership	Self-Monitoring	
		Application		
		Lifelong		
		Reflective		
		Infer		
		Predict		

School library projects give students opportunities for active learning and lend themselves to group work. Traditional research, viewed as an end product, will be transformed by inquiry or action research. Project-based learning developed from real student problem-solving quests is natural to resource-based activities in a school library. Too often, this work is designed for the students—prepackaged and pulled.

As Pat Taylor (1998) states:

If teacher-librarians are really doing this information literacy teaching, why do I only see him/her talking about authors or reading to my child or building castles and talking about fairy tales? Why does my son tell me that he goes to the school library to research from books that the teacher-librarian has put aside for the class . . . that he doesn't have to select any himself? Why is he/she sitting looking at magazines . . . shelving books . . . signing out maps? (p. 1)

Of course, there are many good reasons why we need to do these things, but what are the observable and measurable actions around information literacy in our day-to-day work? If the school library of the future becomes a place where shared experiences and understandings can be facilitated for learners in all stages of development and from all cultures, all stakeholders will need to recognize the importance of information skills in the global world of the next century.

A second pattern or theme arose often during the research: the concept of the learning community. Here was a call for an understanding of the complexity of information literacy to a much wider audience than teacher-librarians. The school library of the future must extend beyond its "walls" and become an integral part of every classroom experience—an extension of the classroom connecting to the diversity in student lives, across curricular boundaries, to other libraries, and community partnerships. School libraries and teacher-librarians must rethink flexible scheduling so that the library is open to students at all times for many purposes. The school library of the future reaches out into the community, connecting learning inside the school to learning outside as well as allowing the world to come in. Some stakeholders thought the library itself might become a smaller facility with students and teachers working in the community. These stakeholders were beginning to discover work in the area of virtual libraries. Others thought it would be a larger facility. Either way, it should be a gateway or interactive hub for the learning community.

To enable this, most stakeholders requested school board policies that support and enable change to be in place and can be supported by administrators and decision-makers. There is much data available—and more needed to be continued and, more importantly, shared—on the impact of school libraries on student achievement (Haycock, 1998; Oberg, 1997). This data needs to be familiar to stakeholder groups so that a common language and understanding ensues, leading to transformational support. Learning experiences focusing on collection development, automated libraries, listservs, Internet searching, brain research, writing a school library plan, and many others need to be developed and/or adapted for stakeholders beyond the field of school library personnel: teachers, administrators, parents, and students.

But this has to go much deeper than board policies or workshops to the postsecondary institutions where not only teacher-librarians need courses on information literacy and resource-based learning but all faculty of education students. The learning experiences offered need to have foundational aspects of active, cooperative learning for adults, model good teaching practices, and have a reflective component. These models include networks, study groups, association involvement, e-mail, listservs, and interactive web sites. Practices such as job shadowing and peer coaching need to be introduced to the understanding of school libraries.

No matter where or with whom I conducted my research, or whatever meetings or forums were held, a third theme of qualified personnel in school libraries, who themselves understand their complexities, became an issue. What is the role of the teacher-librarian? Library assistant? Library technician? Technology teacher? As taxpayers or principals, what are the clear distinctions, besides varied salaries, of these "blurred" roles? Many school library personnel themselves blur the roles, with the key role of teacher-librarian most often being the most misunderstood or practiced.

A teacher-librarian must be a leader in learning who has specialized in postgraduate work in information literacy and how learners learn, using inquiry processes that teach learners how to learn (University of Alberta, 1998). As guides and mediators through the information age—"human interfaces"—teacher-librarians will also plan reflective practices. Teacher-librarians must be continuous learners and change agents, or they could become impediments to equity of opportunity for all students to excellent school library programs. They must have strong skills in collaborative practice to work with teachers to foster shared ownership of the school library and classrooms, moving from cooperative planning to collaborative planning and team teaching. Teacher-librarians can take leadership in construction of knowledge by learning how to pull out underlying structures to enable learners to see connections in learning journeys rather than design them. They must move from controlling people and resources to developing questioning and curious people. Students and staff must be supported, challenged, and trusted.

The fourth resounding pattern or theme evolved around equity, reflecting the findings of the National Symposium on Information, Literacy, and the School Library of Canada (1997), which notes that quality school libraries are a "fundamental right of all children." All students in our rich landscapes of diversity must have access to quality, current resources and programs through partnerships and supports within and beyond school boards. Smaller school libraries need connections with larger ones in community settings as well as public libraries or Internet libraries. Virtual schools need physical spaces for dialogue, discourse, and a myriad of resources that each individual classroom or home cannot provide. In the future, classrooms themselves might disappear as virtual schools flourish, leaving the school library as the point of connection in the community.

The fifth predominant theme of concern to all stakeholders is encompassed in the word "technology." With the rapid technological advancements of the last few years, a great deal of paranoia and confusion has descended upon society at large as well as the educational and library communities. Will technology replace libraries? Are books dead? How will I ever learn how to hook up a network? Save students from the dangers of the Internet? And so on. As I concluded this project, I reflected that the technology theme actually runs through all the others rather than being an entity of its own, which does lead to fragmentation and paranoia.

Therefore, using developmentally sound learning and new thinking processes with technology, learners grow to become information literate as they construct knowledge. Students engaged in active, resource-based learning are equitably entitled to whatever resources or technologies humankind possesses—from ancient manuscripts (some now available on the Internet) to books, software, video, and future cutting-edge technologies, such as virtual reality. We have connected within and beyond our communities using the earliest technologies, such as the "horse and buggy," to go to a place of information or to interact with others. We now continue with global opportunities via chat lines, listservs, virtual seminars, or satellite conferences. Technologies have been available to all through libraries since the advent of the library profession. Technologies, resources, and networks within and beyond schools, both real and virtual, dissolve the isolation factor and misunderstandings that can disempower school library personnel.

Through this project, the action researcher and reflective practitioner developing within me have strengthened confidence in my mission, daily collaborative work, and sharing the research. Venues for sharing have included inventing forums, such as developing mini-conferences with a provincial staff development consortium or system-learning experiences for the broad range of stakeholders. It has also included broadening known venues, such as joining provincial school library and technology associations in a combined conference, and partnering with other associations for national school library conferences and events. Universities and technical institutions in the province report increases in enrollment for school library courses. It is truly becoming a time of transformation, growth, and action where I feel connected to myself as a learner and leader.

CHAPTER 7

Developing a Vision for Your Library and How to Keep It Alive

Your action research might lead to developing a vision for a preferred future for your work. Unlike mission statements about who you are and what you do, a vision pushes the threshold of your current thinking into the distance. What follows is an example of a vision I created after doing my research. The goal was to capture the primary patterns and themes, then put them into a visible framework for transformation.

> **School Libraries of the Future—A Vision Based on Action Research:**
> *Qualified personnel in school library media centers collaboratively develop resource-rich, constructivist environments working with educators, students, and the community. School libraries are vital centers of learning, in both real and virtual time; they are places of human connection, inquiry, and literacies. They are central to the school as learning laboratories, impacting and enhancing teacher and student growth and knowledge. Project-based learning intertwines with curriculum as students are immersed in inquiry, reflecting upon knowledge to make new meaning and enhance application of learning. Equity of access to excellent programs, resources, and leading-edge technologies occurs within this culture and across it to other schools and the global community. Educators facilitate this process in a spirit of inclusion as individuals bring varying cultures, learning styles, personality styles, intelligences, and energy levels to the learning process.*

➡ TIP: Your can create your vision with the stakeholders in your community—your teachers, parents, and students. Using action research, you can determine what is key for your preferred future.

Action research and the excitement of creating a vision need to be followed with strategies that will enable the vision to live and grow. Each part of the vision demands that action plans must be developed and implemented. If your vision involves transforming your school library, you might want to consider the following strategies to get started.

➡ TIP: Organize a school library day involving many stake-holders once or twice per year to build shared understanding.

Choose a theme from your action research. For example, I might choose "community" or "technology." Plan to host a school library day in your school (or a larger school if you do not have room) to save costs on a venue. Consider charging a small fee ($5) to cover coffee, muffins, and a light lunch. Aim for 100 registrants. Organize the day into two or three segments, with four events to choose from in each block. Send registrations out well in advance. Invite teacher-librarians, library support staff, teachers, administrators, and parents. Have students assist as much as possible. Arrange events that will interest all as well as some that will be of special interest to participants. For example, a session on "Introduction to Searching the Internet" might appeal to everyone, whereas a session on "Collection Development in the Electronic Age" might only appeal to librarians. Invite local speakers, especially other teacher-librarians/school library media specialists, to donate their time to present.

➡ TIP: Create and nurture real-time networks.

Being the only teacher-librarian or media specialist in a school can become very lonely and professionally isolating. Consider formalizing a school library network for the purpose of establishing dialogue groups involving the elementary and middle schools that feed into your local high school. Make issues around learning and teaching the priority, and meet approximately every six weeks. Have each school library share host duties. Invite guest presenters and facilitators, as needed, as well as administrators and trustees. Let them know that you are meeting regularly and what it is that you are talking about—creating, sustaining, and celebrating school libraries. Engage in:

- **Experimenting.** Look at current research in school libraries.

- **Examining new models.** See other school libraries; share emerging models.

- **Exploring other environments.** Look at other libraries and public agencies, such as the public library, university libraries, Internet libraries, museums, and art galleries.

- **Sharing.** Projects, units, and ideas.

Begin by surveying the potential network group for "hot topics." Some examples might be: technology and the school library; roles and responsibilities of school library personnel; involving parents in the school library program; working with teachers; cooperative units; creating a school library web page; information literacy; wellness of school library personnel; and so on.

➡ **TIP:** Create and nurture virtual networks.

Although many listservs are available on the Internet, it is a wise idea to create a local listserv. This is another way to build community as well as share expertise in a common area. Day-to-day questions, concerns, and issues that might not be responded to or garner much interest on the larger listservs, such as LM_Net, will often happily be answered from another teacher-librarian in your neighborhood network. Decide on a mandate or theme for the listserv and guidelines for posting.

➡️

TIP: Study the logistics of beginning a task force in your school district or school community to examine the future of school libraries.

What is the governing structure of your school board or school? How can a task force be struck and to what aim? Who will be involved in the task force? How will members be recruited? What are key educational issues in your district or school? How do they affect school libraries or how does the school library affect them?

CHAPTER 8

Adapting the Action Research Model: Student Inquiry

The action research model can be easily adapted to any grade level. Due to the complexity of the process, it might become the student's major project in a unit or, indeed, a project that encompasses the year. Each stage in the process will need to be outlined with the students and teachers. The library and the library staff will need to be scheduled to meet the needs of a class or classes engaging in action research. Following is a sample of a third-grade project based on a science topic: animal life cycles. Any topic could be inserted, and the syntax might change depending on the students' grade level. It is outlined in a series of addresses to the students. Suggested pre-lessons appear prior to the student discourse; depending on your school library program, you might have covered these lessons with the students or will need to as the process progresses. Many of these lessons are available in sources from references listed, including my previous book: *Library Centers, Teaching Information Literacy, Skills, and Processes* (Libraries Unlimited, 1997). An action research checklist for students follows this section.

Pre-research

➡ TIP: Pre-lesson: Using graphic organizers (webbing).

Does this sound familiar to you?: We are going to be working on a library research project for the next two weeks. You can choose one animal's life cycle to research. You will find out about its food, habitat, enemies, appearance, and babies. You will answer the questions from the handout and include a drawing. It needs to be completed in two weeks.

So, where do you start? What do you do? The book you might read or be reading about your favorite animal does not seem to be neatly divided into the topics or questions that are asked for. Three more books and an encyclopedia article answered a few questions, but you cannot locate the others. And your Internet search on your animal turned up 55,000 sites. That is a lot to cover in two weeks!

By this time, you are ready to groan about the research. But do you know that some people spend their whole life doing research and that it is very exciting? Think about scientists, doctors, explorers, and authors and all of their discoveries and stories.

Is research starting to sound a little more exciting? Perhaps looking at your topic in a new way will lead you to interesting and important discoveries by putting "action" into your research.

What is "action research"? It involves you as the researcher, the scientist, the investigator. You work through a series of steps that lead you to deep under-standings about your topics, new discoveries, and your own ideas and opinions. And the best thing—you are not alone! Action research will have you working with many people in many ways. Finally, action research is not neat and tidy—there are many twists and turns in research that take you from one idea to another; that change your mind on many aspects about your topic. Let's use action research to find out more about animal life cycles.

You will need to have a small notebook or journal for the action research project. Think of this notebook or journal the way a scientist thinks of the notebook that he or she records information in as he or she investigates something. The notes in this notebook are known as "field notes."

First of all, write the name of your topic in the center of a page in your notebook or journal, then draw a circle around it. Write as much as you can about what you know or think you know about the topic. This is a "mind map" or "web." We will do this without any books or other materials around. Like the scientist, you will test some of your ideas as you do your research. Write some questions that come to mind on the back of the paper.

Make a list of all the places or people that you think could help you find information about the topic. Your paper should look quite messy by now.

I: Context

➡️ TIP: Pre-lessons: Broadening and narrowing the topic; developing key or essential questions (McKenzie, 1997).

*Next, we are going to put our ideas into **context**. This means it is time to make a decision and description about the size of your investigation. How big will your study be? Will it focus on animals in our area or in other parts of the world? Will it be research into one species of your animal or a number of different species? For example, one species of frog, bat, or shark or many or all species? Is there anyone you know who might be an expert on your animal or any place you could visit or write to about the animal's life cycle?*

II: Issue

➡️ TIP: Pre-lesson: Review on developing key questions.

*Once you have made this decision, look back at that messy "mind map." You have written things that you know or think you know about your animal's life cycle, and you have also written some questions. What do you think is the most important question? This most important question should be something you really wonder about your topic—a key **issue**. For example, is your animal's life cycle threatened or interrupted due to dangers in the environment? What is the relationship between your animal and humans?*

This most important question is a question that you will come back to and search for as you investigate the topic. It is a question that might lead you to other information that you had not thought about. It is a question that keeps you interested in knowing more. Keep it in mind at all times as you continue your research. Now, back to that messy piece of paper . . .

III: Resources

➡️ TIP: Pre-lessons: Finding books and other sources; creating bibliographies (Sykes, 1997); effective Internet searching.

We are now ready to search the school library media center to locate current **resources** *that match your topic. Current nonfiction books will bring you up-to-date on developments or knowledge about the topic. Authors of these books have saved you a lot of time by researching books and other sources already. It is also a good idea to try to look through at least three books about your animal to see how different authors have approached the subject and how their findings compare.*

The Internet is a wonderful research tool. It has a lot of researched material but also lots of opinions, such as reports by other students. It could also have a site about your animal by scientists who study it. You might need assistance to help you search efficiently and effectively. For example, if you type in your animal, such as "frogs," you'll come up with those 55,000 sites! The Internet can give you daily information and opinions, but a book usually takes two years to write and research. Compare sources! You might also find a video, brochure, or other resource in the library to help you sort out fact from fiction.

After reading or skimming through your books or web sites or watching videos, you probably have a few notes and are getting a good picture about your animal's life cycle. Do not forget to write the title, author, and year of your resources, even for Internet sources, as you go along. Later, when you must finish, your list of resources or bibliography will be almost done.

IV: Goals, Outcomes, Action Plans

➡️ TIP: Pre-lessons: Setting goals; hypothesizing; planning tools.

*Now that you know much more about your topic, look back again at that messy "mind map." Did you read or learn about something that you had written a question about? Did you come up with new ideas to add? Take a few moments to decide where you are going to focus your action research—these are **goals**. Think about writing one or two goals. Did you come across a particular species or information about your animal's life cycle that you would like to know more about? Did you read about your animal in danger and wonder what is happening today to help the animal's life cycle? For whatever goals you write, decide exactly what you are trying to discover— what the **outcomes** might be. If you are studying a certain species, do you wonder how they are the same or different from other species? If you are intrigued by a danger to the animal, could you find out how to help? Now is the time to make some **action plans**. You need to talk to other people and begin an action research journey!*

V: Journey Events

➡️ TIP: Pre-lessons: Conducting an interview or survey.

*What kind of **journey events** will help you investigate your topic first-hand? First of all, talk to your teacher, teacher-librarian/media specialist, and parents. They might know or share their opinions with you about your animal's life cycle. Or they might be able to help you locate and interview a local expert at a zoo, wildlife sanctuary, library, museum, university, or science center. Your classmates can also help with the action journey. Survey other students for their impressions or knowledge about your animal and its life cycle.*

"Experts" can also be a keystroke away—many scientists, museum experts, and university experts respond to student questions on e-mail or on the telephone. No matter how you interview a person, make sure you have an adult helping you for safety reasons. Librarians and teachers volunteer to run sites, such as "AskERICforKids," and will help you research your topic online. Whether in real or virtual time, make sure you are always brief and polite. Write an introduction to your interview that includes who you are, what school and grade you represent, and what topic you are researching. State how you were put into contact with the person you are interviewing and how grateful you are for their help. Write out at least five questions to ask your subject about your topic. Conclude by asking the subject if they have any additional information they might want to add and thank them again for the interview. Offer to mail or e-mail them a copy of the interview in case they want to add anything or check that they were properly quoted.

If your interview is in person or on the telephone, practice ahead of time to write quick and short notes that summarize what the person has said. If possible, and with the subject's permission, you might want to tape record the interview and listen to it later for summarizing.

VI: Patterns/Themes

➡ TIP: Pre-lessons: Finding key words or phrases; project ideas for sharing and reflection.

By this time, you should have a lot of field notes about your topic from books, experts, and maybe even your friends, parents, or neighbors. You might have found the answers you were seeking or you might have discovered something new. There is one more "action" step.

*Using a highlighter, read through your notes and emphasize what you think are the most important points that answer your questions. You are looking for **patterns** or **themes** to develop. What seems to be common about the animal's life cycle, no matter where you read, saw, or heard about it? When you find these key patterns or themes, those are the findings you need to group. When they are grouped together, you are ready to analyze what you have discovered. What conclusions have you come to or discovered about this topic? What did you learn? How will you represent your action research? By making a poster? Writing a play? Making a model?*

ACTION RESEARCH CHECKLIST

☐ MIND MAP

☐ CONTEXT

☐ ISSUE

☐ RESOURCES

☐ GOALS

☐ OUTCOMES

☐ PLAN

☐ JOURNEY EVENTS

☐ PATTERNS/THEMES

☐ CONCLUSION

☐ BIBLIOGRAPHY

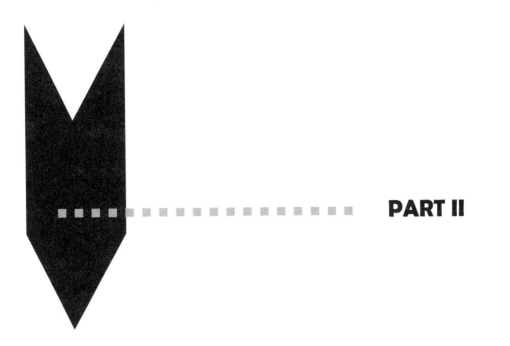

PART II

Presentation (also on CD-ROM)

The following PowerPoint presentation has been adapted from the research and can be shared with your school community, school board, university class, or other interest group to build background and explore issues around the future of school libraries.

School Libraries of the Future

What kind of place will the school library of the future be?

- Will it indeed be a place or a center for knowledge construction?

- ...a place of connection?

- ...a physical or virtual place or a blend?

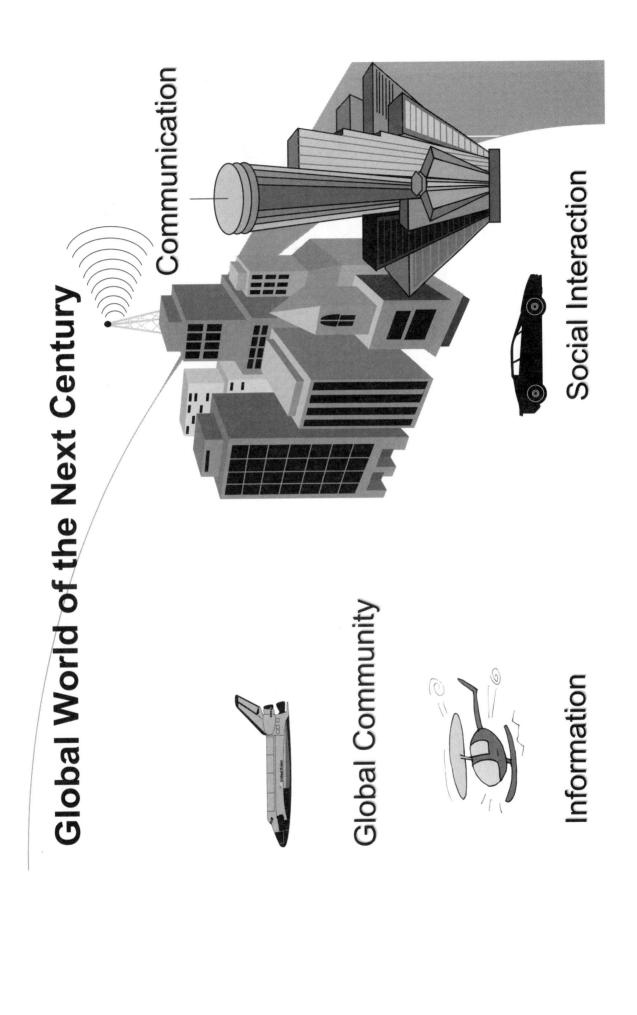

STUDENT IDEAS...

- more computers
- scanner
- better printers
- Digi-Pad (to draw)
- real card catalog
- virtual glove
- reading carousel
- comfortable chairs
- more sci-fi
- more Jane Goodall

- easier to see (open spaces)
- microfiche reader (for old newspapers)
- knapsack section
- sound-field barrier
- intelligence computer
- voice command
- fax machine (Internet fax from Library of Congress)
- CNN hookup
- working water fountain
- Albert Einstein's Theory of Relativity in a book

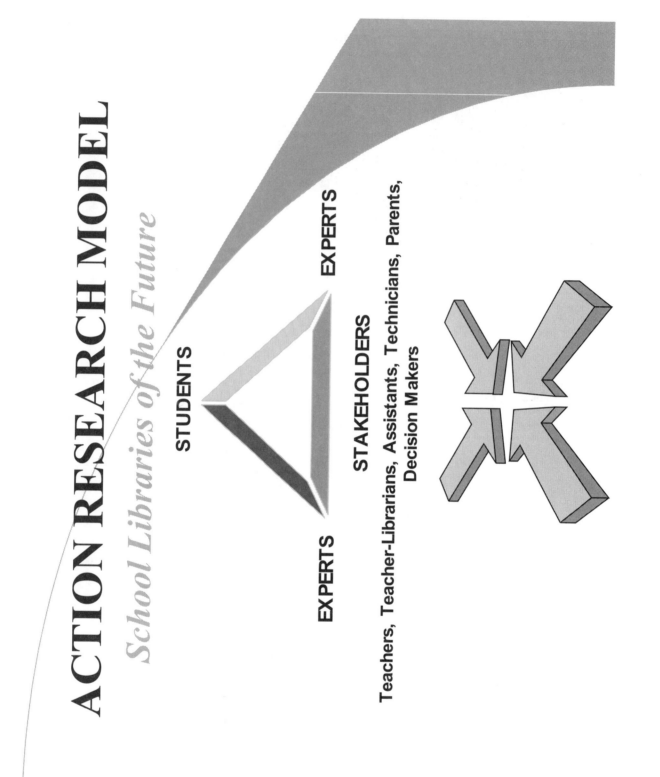

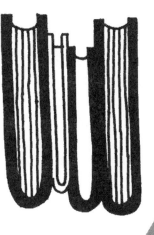

CONTEXT

University of Portland Research Project:

- school libraries regionally
- school libraries in a large metropolitan district

CONTEXT

Explore current practices for future school libraries to address:

- role of the school library on learning
- reduction of personnel
- erosion of collections
- equity of opportunity in local and global communities

ISSUE OR "HUNCH"

School libraries will serve to create independent, lifelong learners who can prepare themselves to use ideas and information:

- interact with it
- restructure it
- create from it
- communicate
- reflect

ISSUE OR "HUNCH"

School libraries will:

- stand for intellectual freedom as democratic institutions where viewpoints are presented objectively and materials are available without cost

- comprise foundation aspects of school improvement plans and whole-school culture

- be places of active learning that exemplify the definition of collaboration among all stakeholders

ISSUE OR "HUNCH"

Vision

I believe:

- that school libraries of the future will be vital centers of constructivist learning in both real and virtual time

- *Clear Vision + Action = Transformation*

WHAT THE LITERATURE REVEALS

"Libraries are good things, and the people who work in them do good work..."

… Knowledge and understanding, not data and information, are central with an ethical mission of equality of access to materials and resources for all. We should take pride in the way librarians have honored this mission for centuries and accept the weight of that mission."

Crawford, Walt, and Michael Gorman. *Future Libraries: Dreams, Madness & Reality*. Chicago, IL: American Library Association, 1994.

WHAT THE LITERATURE REVEALS

Futurists write that citizens of tomorrow must become adept questioners and critical users of information.

"In a digital world new thinking processes will need to be developed as new technologies emerge."

Negroponte, Nicholas. *Being Digital*. USA: Vintage, 1995.

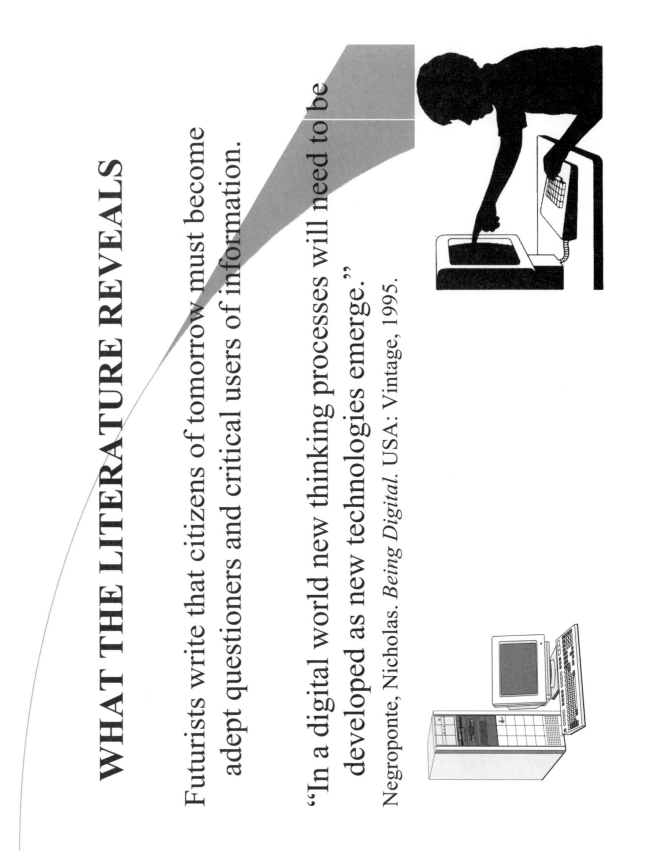

WHAT THE LITERATURE REVEALS

"We will need to move from hierarchical, competitive societies to supportive, collaborative, interactive cultures."

de Kerckhove, Derrick. *The Skin of Culture: Investigating the New Electronic Reality*. Toronto, ON: Somerville House, 1995.

WHAT THE LITERATURE REVEALS

"Latin *educare*, meaning to raise and nurture, is more a matter of imparting values and critical faculties than inputting raw data. Education is about enlightenment, not just access."

Shenk, David. *Data Smog: Surviving the Information Glut.* San Francisco: Harper Edge, 1996.

WHAT THE LITERATURE REVEALS

"Plans for future school libraries need to be flexible and open, preparing lifelong learners for their future and not this generation's past. Reading will change in two ways: breadth and depth; kids need to *make* answers not find them to change the traditional research paradigm."

McKenzie, Jamie. "Deep Thinking and Deep Reading in an Age of Info-Glut, Info-Garbage, Info-Glitz, and Info-Glimmer," *From Now On Electronic Journal* 6(6) (1997). Available http://www.fno.org

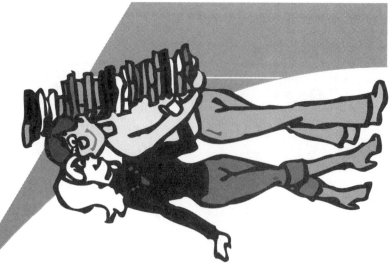

WHAT THE LITERATURE REVEALS

"The school library program of the future needs to be student centered so that students become:

- avid readers,
- critical and creative thinkers,
- interested learners,
- organized investigators,
- effective communicators,
- responsible information users,
- skilled users of technology."

Loertscher, David. "A Farewell Challenge," *School Library Media Quarterly*, 24 (4): 192–94 (1996).

FOCUS OF JOURNEY

Research Tools:

- literature
- telephone interviews
- surveys
- focus groups

FOCUS OF JOURNEY

Experts:

- Joy McGregor: Assistant Professor, School of Library and Information Studies, Texas Woman's University

- Ken Haycock: Dean, Information and Archival Sciences, University of British Columbia

- Pam Horan: University of Portland, Off-Campus Library Services/Graduate Students

- Dianne Oberg: University of Alberta, School of Information Sciences

- Pat Taylor: President, Association for Teacher-Librarians of Canada

- Barbara Stripling: President, American Association of School Libraries

FOCUS OF JOURNEY

Stakeholders:

- teachers
- teacher-librarians
- library assistants and technicians
- parents
- school and district administrators
- student focus groups

Describe the characteristics that depict an excellent school library of the twenty-first century.

PATTERNS AND THEMES

Equity of access:

- to quality resources
- to current resources
- to the use of resources

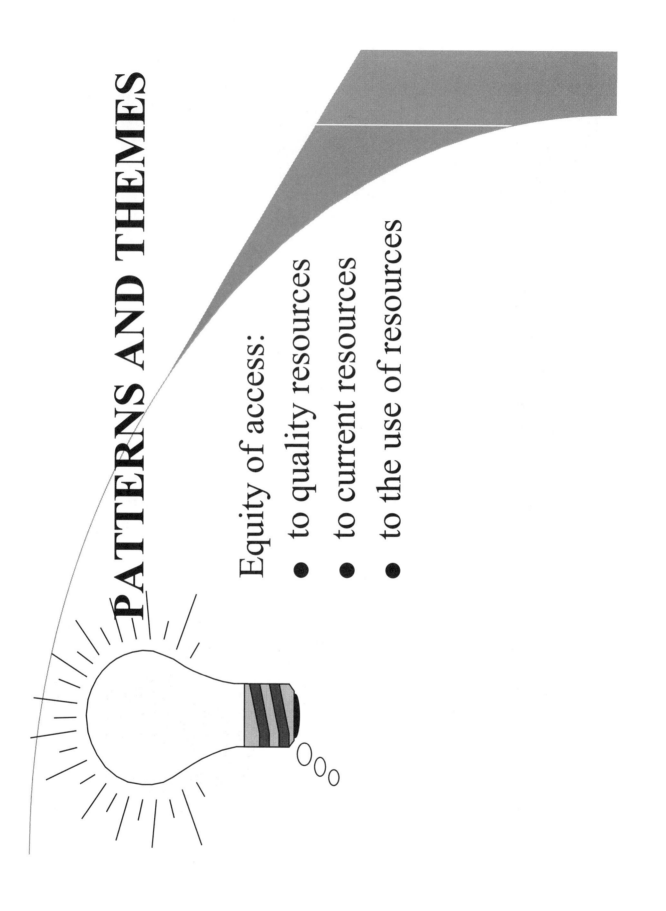

CONSTRUCTIVISM

Construct Knowledge:

- ideas
- information

CONSTRUCTIVISM

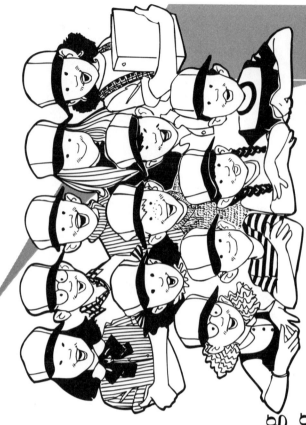

Future Libraries:

- will transform from collectors and disseminators to "information creators"

- will move from the control of people and resources to developing curious and questioning people . . . .

- will focus on shared experiences and understandings for learners in all learning styles and developmental stages, and from all cultures

TECHNOLOGY

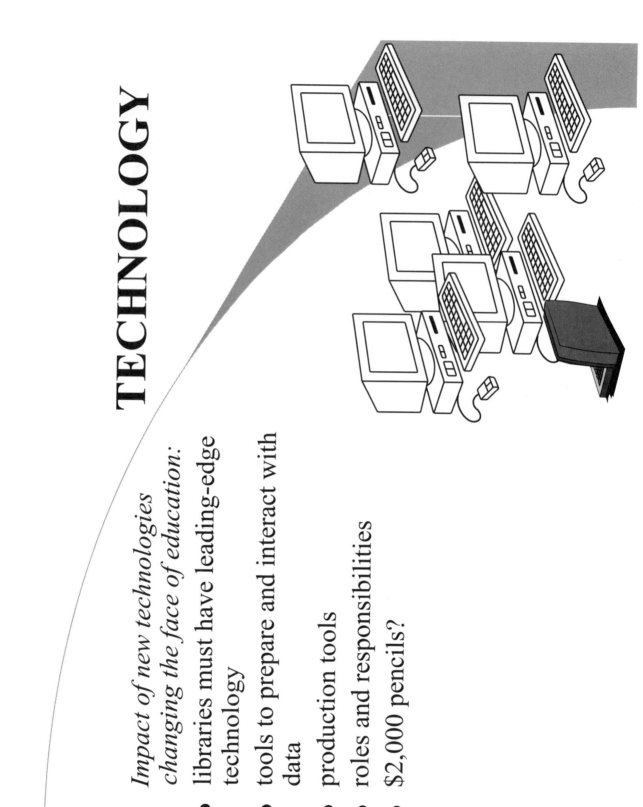

Impact of new technologies changing the face of education:

- libraries must have leading-edge technology

- tools to prepare and interact with data

- production tools

- roles and responsibilities

- $2,000 pencils?

TECHNOLOGY

Automated Libraries:

- Online Public Access Catalogs (OPACs)
- automated circulation systems
- CD-ROMs
- Internet

COMMUNITY

- Info-center or hub of the school connecting learning to the world and allowing the world to come in

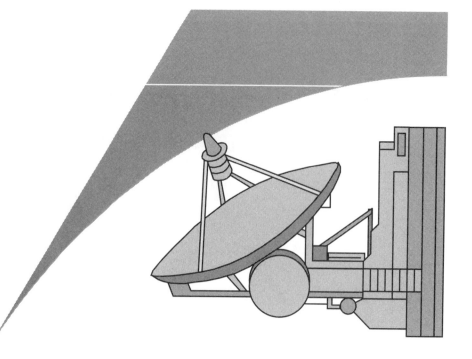

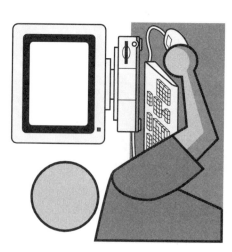

COMMUNITY

- a model for work outside of the school

- an extension of the classroom connecting to student lives, across curricular boundaries, to other libraries, and community partnerships

COMMUNITY

The school library of the future must:

- extend beyond its "walls" and become an integral part of every classroom experience.

- rethink flexible scheduling so that the library is open to students at all times for many purposes.

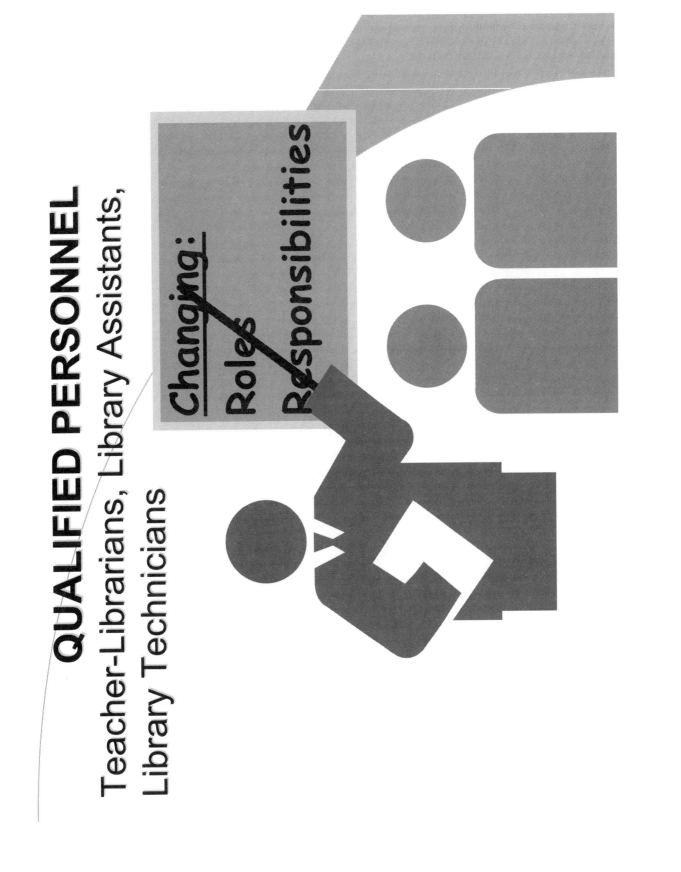

QUALIFIED PERSONNEL

- must themselves understand their roles and the complexities of the school library learning environment
- must work as teams in support of student learning

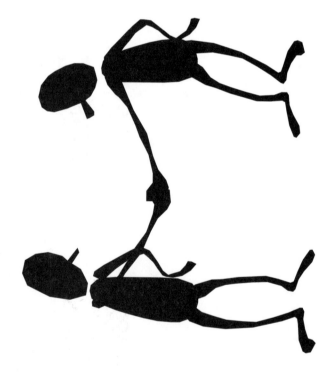

*What is important
about the relationship
of school libraries to
learning and teaching?*

INFORMATION LITERACY

- processes of critical thinking

- reading in all formats

- learning how to learn

- action research: begin with a problem or question

RESOURCE-BASED LEARNING

Learners need opportunities:

- to select the best information
- to put facts into construction
- to work together to solve problems
- to create

PROJECT-BASED LEARNING

- Project-based learning is natural to resource-based activities in the school library.

- School library projects give students opportunities for active learning and lend themselves to *cooperative group* work.

INTERDISCIPLINARY

- school libraries are sources of complexity in learning

- connections of knowledge; between and beyond "subjects"

- drawing conclusions

LEARNING

- School is student's "work."

- Learning in the social experience is the definition of collaboration.

LEARNING

What does this look like in practice?

LEARNING

Inquiry:

- students form questions
- questions are our primary technological tool

McKenzie, Jamie.
fno.org/Oct97/question.html

LEARNING

Dialoguing:

- discussion groups

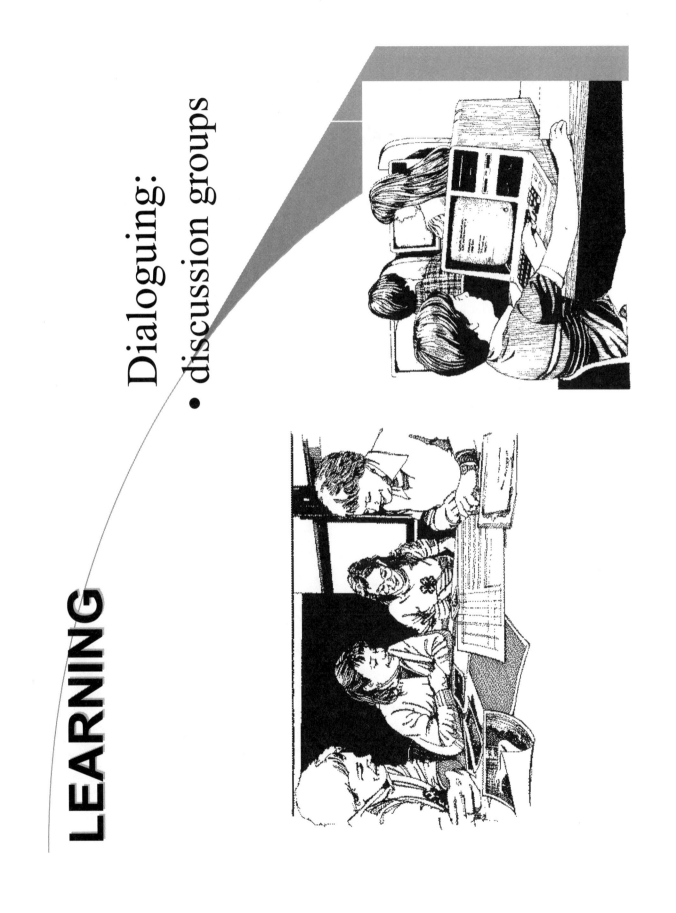

LEARNING COACHING

LEARNING

Reflection:
- reading
- portfolios
- student-led conferences
- rubrics
- performances
- exhibits
- observations
- journals
- celebrations

LEARNING

Technology:

- we do not read the same way
- learn and relearn
- making order out of chaos

Students must be supported, challenged, and trusted.

LEARNING

Teacher-librarians:

- learning leaders: experts in current learning knowledge
- mentors
- staff developers
- guide/mediator/facilitator through information age
- continuous learners
- collaborative practitioners

Describe the impediments to equitable access to excellent school libraries.

IMPEDIMENTS

- gap between resources and technology
- lack of technical support
- effects of school libraries on achievement
- non-flexible scheduling
- need for active administrative support
- teacher-librarians who are not learning leaders

How might
some of these
impediments
be overcome?

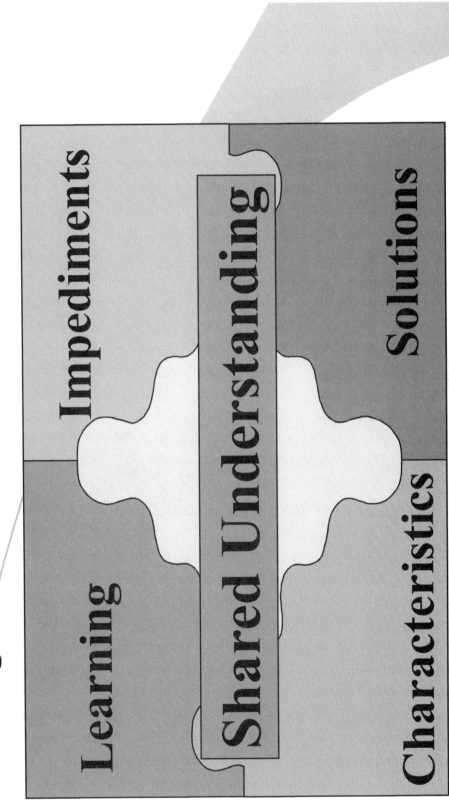

All Stakeholders...

...need to recognize the importance of information/communication knowledge in the global world of the future.

OVERCOMING IMPEDIMENTS

- qualified personnel: university/technical courses in school libraries

- staff development for school library teams

- teacher-librarians as instructional leaders

- teachers experiencing learning in the way we want them to team and teach

- shared understanding of the complexities of the school library plan

- program-based budgets and seeking grants

NEW STAFF DEVELOPMENT MODELS

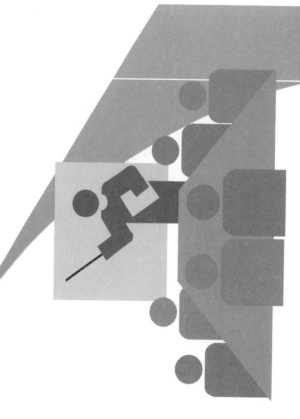

- job shadow
- job share ("best practice")
- peer coaching
- mini-conferences

NETWORKS

- study groups
- e-mail
- listservs
- virtual seminars
- interactive web sites

COLLABORATIVE PLANNING

- focus on student learning
- "our resources"
- acceptance as equals

COLLABORATION

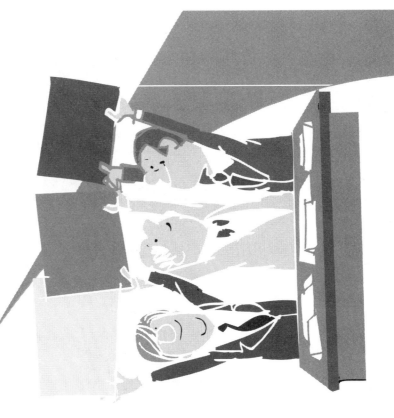

- all viewpoints presented
- might not always agree
- strive to build consensus around practice

COLLABORATION

- School Library
- Teams
- Team Teaching

TEAMS

- share joint experiences and labor

- are more creative

- provide honest, constructive feedback

- share operation/support of school library experiences

The National Symposium on Information Literacy and the School Library in Canada:

- The school library belongs to everyone as an integral part of the fundamental quality of our schools and a fundamental right of all children in Canada.

Snowball effect of action research:

- many research "leads"

- more focus groups

- increase in upgrading school library collections and personnel

- increased interest/enrollment in graduate and technical school library courses

CONCLUSION

"The library is becoming an increasingly dumb place to store information. It doesn't make much sense to use the planet's resources to do that. It doesn't make much sense for trees to die for the purpose of disseminating information...

...Librarians should understand that what they do is create space, **cognitive space**, in the environment. It can look like a public library, a web site...or whatever......

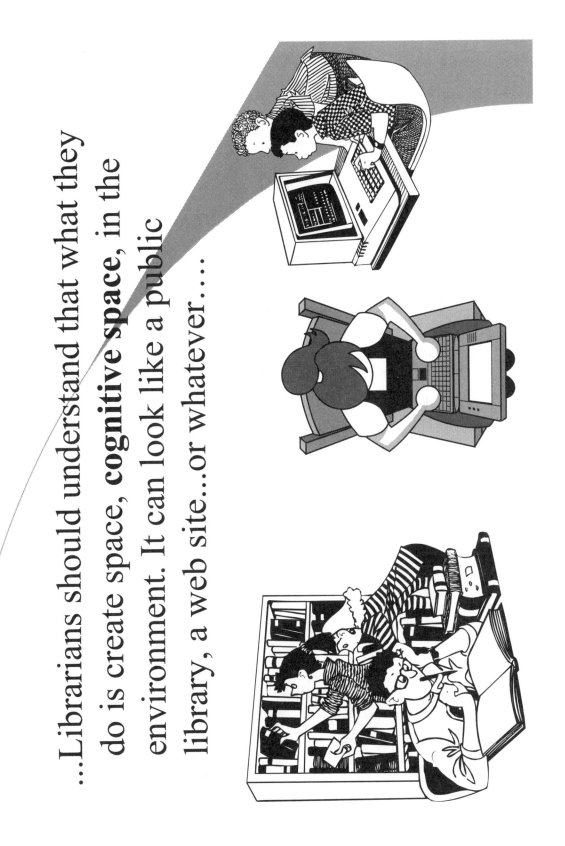

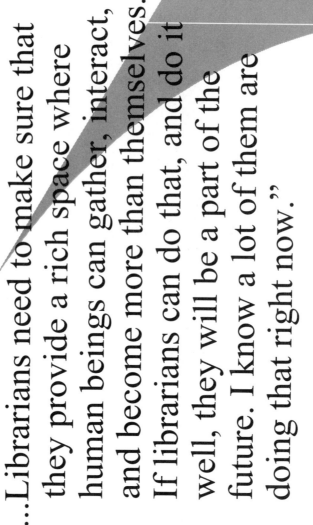

"...Librarians need to make sure that they provide a rich space where human beings can gather, interact, and become more than themselves. If librarians can do that, and do it well, they will be a part of the future. I know a lot of them are doing that right now."

John Perry Barlow

Chepesiuk, Ron. "Librarians As Cyberspace Guerrillas," *American Libraries* 27 (8): 49–51 (1996).

Bibliography

Alberta Education. "Learner Outcomes in Information and Communication Technology ECS–12," 1997. Available: http://ednet.edc.gov.ab.ca/ict/pofs.asp

American Association of School Libraries and Association for Educational Communication and Technology. "Information Literacy Standards for Student Learning," 1997. Available: http://www.infolit.org/definitions/9standards.htm

American Association of School Libraries and Association for Educational Communication and Technology. *Information Power: Guidelines for School Library Media Programs.* Chicago, IL: American Association of School Libraries. Washington, DC: Association for Educational Communication and Technology, 1988.

Anderson, Gary L., Kathryn Herr, and Ann Sigrid Nihlen. *Studying Your Own School: An Educator's Guide to Qualitative Practitioner Research.* Thousand Oaks, CA: Corwin Press, 1994.

Anderson, Robert L. *Intellectual Development in the Piagetian System.* (Educative Concepts). Portland, OR: University of Portland, School of Education, 1996.

———. *A Learner-Centered, Integration Design.* (Educative Concepts). Portland, OR: University of Portland, School of Education, 1996.

———. *Structures, Groupings, and the Great Constructs of Human Inquiry.* (Educative Concepts). Portland, OR: University of Portland, School of Education, 1996.

Aronson, Marc. "Not a Necessary Purchase: The Journals Judged," *The Horn Book Magazine* 73 (4): 27–43 (1997).

Association for Teacher-Librarianship in Canada and Canadian School Library Association. "Students' Information Literacy Needs in the 21st Century: Competencies for Teacher-Librarians," 1997. Available: www.atlc.ca

Beane, James A. "Curriculum Integration and the Disciplines of Knowledge," *Phi Delta Kappan* 76 (8): 616–22 (1995).

Bens, Shirley. "Technology and the Changing Role of Teacher-Librarians," 1997. Available at: http://www.11ed.educ.ubc.ca/libe/integrated.htm

Benton Foundation. "Buildings, Books, and Bytes: Libraries and Communities in the Digital Age," 1996. Available: http://www.benton.org/Library/Kellogg/buildings.html

Berra, Yogi. Quotation from http://www.tpub.com/Quotes/b.htm

Brandt, Ron. "On Using Knowledge About Our Brain: A Conversation with Bob Sylwester," *Educational Leadership* 54 (6): 16–19 (1997).

Calgary Board of Education. "The Collection Development Plan: Revision of Section 10," *The Teacher-Librarian Resource Manual*. Calgary, AB: Calgary Board of Education, 1998.

———. "Growth and Improvement: Expectations for School Library Programs in the Calgary Board of Education." Calgary, AB: Calgary Board of Education, 1990.

———. "Guidelines for Evaluation of Learning Resources: Revision." Calgary, AB: Calgary Board of Education, 1998.

———. "Report of the Regular Board Meeting September 25, 1990." Calgary, AB: Calgary Board of Education, 1990.

———. "Resource Centre Program Policy 3,012: 3rd Amendment." Calgary, AB: Calgary Board of Education, 1985.

———. "Quality Learning Document." Calgary, AB: Calgary Board of Education, 1997.

———. "The School Library Program." Calgary, AB: Calgary Board of Education, 1990.

———. *The Teacher-Librarian Resource Manual*. Calgary, AB: Calgary Board of Education, 1991.

California School Library Association. *From Library Skills to Information Literacy: A Handbook for the 21st Century*. Castle Rock, CO: Hi Willow Research and Publishing, 1997.

Canadian Library Association. "Strategic Plan Draft." Ottawa, ON: Canadian Library Association, 1998.

Cavill, Patricia M. *Report: Changes in the Public and School Library Market*. Pat Cavill Consulting, Calgary: AB, 1997.

Chepesiuk, Ron. "Librarians As Cyberspace Guerrillas," *American Libraries* 27 (8): 49–51 (1996).

Cohen, Philip. "Developing Information Literacy: Advocates Promote Resource-Based Learning," *ASCD Education Update* 37 (2): 1, 3, 8 (1995).

Crawford, Walt, and Michael Gorman. *Future Libraries: Dreams, Madness & Reality*. Chicago, IL: American Library Association, 1994.

de Kerckhove, Derrick. *The Skin of Culture: Investigating the New Electronic Reality*. Toronto, ON: Somerville House, 1995.

Doiron, Ray, and Judy Davies. *Partners in Learning: Students, Teachers, and the School Library.* Englewood, CO: Libraries Unlimited, 1998.

———. *Reflection and Renewal in Prince Edward Island School Libraries.* Charlottetown, PE: Department of Education, 1996.

———. "School Library Resource Centre Policies in Canada: Re-Viewing a Shared Vision." Paper presented at the American Educational Research Association Annual Conference held in Chicago, IL. March 1997.

Doyle, Christina S. "Information Literacy in an Information Society: A Concept for the Information Age." East Lansing, MI: National Center for Research on Teacher Learning, 1994.

Edmonton Public Schools. "What Role Do School Libraries Play in Technology Integration?" 1997. Available: http://www.epsb.ca

Edwards, Gail. "Looking at Ourselves, Looking at Others: Multiculturalism in Canadian Children's Picture Books." Paper presented at the conference of The International Association of School Librarianship and The Association for Teacher-Librarianship in Canada held in Vancouver, BC. July 1996.

Eisenberg, Michael, and Robert Berkowitz. *Information Problem Solving: The Big Six Skills Approach to Library and Information Skills Instruction.* Norwood, NJ: Ablex, 1990.

Gauntley, Tim, producer/director. *School Libraries 2000: Discovering the Information Age Together* (video), 1997. Available from Multimedia Support Services, Toronto District School Board, 155 College St., Toronto, ON, M5T 1P6, Canada.

Hamilton, Donald. "Mission in Action," *Quill and Quire* 60 (10): 24 (1994).

———. "School Libraries for Tomorrow," *Impact* 7 (2): 6–8 (1998).

Harrington-Lueker, Donna. "Cybrarians and the Powered-up Library," *Electronic Learning* 16 (6): 44–49 (1997).

Haycock, Ken. "Connected: School Libraries at the Millennium." Keynote address presented at the conference of The Prince Edward Island Teacher-Librarian Association and The Association for Teacher-Librarianship in Canada held in Charlottetown, PE. May 1998.

———. "Reinventing School Libraries: Alternatives, Models and Options for the Future," *Education Canada* 38 (1): 44–52 (1997).

Haycock, Ken, and Lynn Lighthall, eds. *Information Rich but Knowledge Poor? Emerging Issues for Schools and Libraries Worldwide.* Seattle, WA: International Association of School Librarianship, 1997.

Johnson, Doug. *The Indispensable Librarian: Surviving and Thriving in School Media Centers in the Information Age.* Worthington, OH: Linworth, 1997.

Johnson, Doug, and Michael Eisenberg. "Computer Literacy and Information Literacy: A Natural Combination," *Emergency Librarian* 23 (5): 12–16 (1996).

Kagan, Spencer. "The Structural Approach to Cooperative Learning," *Educational Leadership* 47 (4): 12–15 (1990).

Kelly, Barbara. "Forging Forward." Symposium conducted on Information, Literacy and the School Library of Canada held in Ottawa, ON. November 1997.

Killion, Joellen, and Cindy Harrison. "The Multiple Roles of Staff Developers," *Journal of Staff Development* 18 (3): 34–44 (1997).

Lance, Keith Curry, Lynda Welborn, and Christine Hamilton-Pennell. *The Impact of School Library Media Centers on Academic Achievement.* Castle Rock, CO: Hi Willow Research and Publishing, 1993.

Langford, Linda. "Information Literacy: A Clarification," *School Libraries Worldwide* 4 (1): 59–72 (1998).

Ledwell, Carolyn. *Building Better Learners: A Parent's Guide to Preparing Students for the Information Age Using the School Library Program.* Vancouver, BC: Association for Teacher-Librariarship in Canada, 1998.

Leiberman, Ann. "Practices That Support Teacher Development: Transforming Conceptions of Professional Learning," *Phi Delta Kappan* 76 (8): 591–96 (1995).

Loertscher, David. "A Farewell Challenge," *School Library Media Quarterly* 24 (4): 192–94 (1996).

——. "The Future School Library Media Center," *School Library Media Annual* 13: 78–90 (1995).

——. "Information Literacy for Today and Tomorrow." Paper presented at the conference of The International Association of School Librarianship and The Association for Teacher-Librarianship in Canada held in Vancouver, BC. July 1997.

Lupton, Paul. "Recent Happenings and Future Developments: Teacher-Librarians in an Information Rich World." Paper presented at the conference of The International Association of School Librarianship and The Association for Teacher-Librarianship in Canada held in Vancouver, BC. July 1997.

Manning, Patricia. "When Less is More: Cultivating a Healthy Collection," *School Library Journal* 43 (5): 54–55 (1997).

McKenzie, Jamie. "Deep Thinking and Deep Reading in an Age of Info-Glut, Info-Garbage, Info-Glitz and Info-Glimmer," *From Now On Electronic Journal* 6 (6) (1997a). Available: http://www.fno.org

——. "Framing Essential Questions," *From Now On Electronic Journal* 6 (1) (1996a). Available: http://www.fno.org

———. "Libraries of the Future," *School Libraries in Canada* 16 (2): 6–9 (1996b).

———. "Making WEB Meaning," *Educational Leadership* 54 (3): 30–32 (1996c).

———. "The Post-Modem School in the New Information Landscape," *From Now On Electronic Journal* 6 (2) (1996d). Available: http://www.fno.org

———. "A Questioning Toolkit," *From Now On Electronic Journal* 7 (3) (1997b). Available: http://questioning.org/Q7/toolkit.html

Moursand, David. "The Emerging Global Library," *Learning and Leading with Technology* 24 (2): 4–5 (1997).

Musgrove, Penny. "Re-Create Your Media Center and Program," *MultiMedia Schools* 4 (3): 16–20 (1997).

Negroponte, Nicholas. *Being Digital*. USA: Vintage, 1995.

November, Alan. "From Smart Toilets to Smart Schools." Speech presented during the 14th Annual National Effective Schools Conference held in Phoenix, AZ. February 1997.

Oberg, Dianne. "Assembly Report," *International Association of School Librarianship* 27 (1): 18–24 (1998).

———. "Ways of Demonstrating That School Libraries Make a Difference in Learning," *LRC Newsletter* Fall: 18–22 (1997).

Ontario School Library Association. "Information Studies Grades 1–12." Toronto, ON: Ontario School Library Association, 1998.

Pappas, Marjorie L. "Library Media Specialists and Teachers in the School of Tomorrow," *School Library Media Activities Monthly* 13 (8): 32–34, 1997.

Peat, David, Robert Mulcahy, and Lorraine Wilgosh. "Learning Resources Evaluation: A Considerate Framework for Educators," *Education Canada* 37 (1): 15–19, 51 (1997).

Pennell, Victoria, ed. *Information Literacy: An Advocacy Kit for Teacher-Librarians*. North Vancouver, BC: Association for Teacher-Librarianship in Canada, 1996.

Richardson, Paul. "Students As Researchers in the Information Age," *The Australian Journal of Language and Literacy* 19 (4): 372–76 (1996).

Roberts, Linda. "A Long Way to Go," *Technology Connection* 3 (5): 15–17 (1996).

Rockfield, Gary. "Beyond Library Power: Can Schools and Public Libraries Collaborate?," *School Library Journal* 44 (1): 30–33 (1998).

Shenk, David. *Data Smog: Surviving the Information Glut*. San Francisco: Harper Edge, 1996.

Stapinski, Helene. "Data Delirium," *People* 11 (3): 145–46 (1997).

Stripling, Barbara. "School Libraries: Catalysts for Authentic Learning," *School Library Media Quarterly* 25 (2): 89–90 (1997).

Sykes, Judith. *Library Centers: Teaching Information Literacy, Skills, and Processes: K–6*. Englewood, CO: Libraries Unlimited, 1997.

Sylwester, Robert. "The Role of the Arts on Brain Development and Maintenance." Paper presented at the conference of the Alberta Association of Supervision and Curriculum Development held in Calgary, AB. April 1998.

Taylor, Pat. "Only Connect: Marion the Librarian at the Millennium." Plenary session presented at the conference of The Prince Edward Island Teacher-Librarian Association and The Association for Teacher-Librarianship in Canada, held in Charlottetown, PE. 1998.

———. "President's Message," *Impact* 7 (3): 1–2 (1998).

Toffler, Alvin. Quotation from http://www.quotationspage.com/search.php3

University of Alberta. "Teacher-Librarianship by Distance Learning," 1998. Available: http://www.quasar.ualberta.ca/tl-dl/

University of Calgary. "Library of the Future Task Force," 1998. Available: http://www.ucalgary.ca/library/lftf/index.html

U.S. Department of Labor. (2000). "What Work Requires of Schools: A SCANS Report for America 2000." The Secretary's Commission on Achieving Necessary Skills, 2000. Available: http://www.academicinnovations.com/report.html

Woolls, Blanche. "A Contract for Success," *School Library Journal* 41 (9): 140 (1995).

———. "Helping Teachers Sustain the Vision," *Emergency Librarian* 25 (1): 14–18 (1997).

Index